THE BATTLE OF
TOURMAKEADY
FACT OR FICTION

But now I shall tell you the Truth

The Book of Daniel 11:2

Praise the Lord Jesus Christ
This book is also dedicated to my wife Céline and our daughters
Aoife, Clíodhna and Doireann, whose support, patience and
tolerance are greatly appreciated.

The Battle of
TOURMAKEADY
Fact or Fiction

A Study of the
IRA Ambush
and its
Aftermath

CAPTAIN
DONAL BUCKLEY

NONSUCH

First published 2008

Nonsuch Publishing
73 Lower Leeson Street
Dublin 2, Ireland
www.nonsuchireland.com

British Library Cataloguing in Publication Data.
A catalogue record for this book is available from the British Library.

ISBN 978 1 84588 926 5

Typesetting and origination by The History Press Ltd
Printed and bound in Great Britain

Contents

Acknowledgements

I would like to acknowledge the invaluable assistance of a number of individuals without whose advice the writing of this book would not have been possible. This book is based on a thesis which I submitted for my MA History in the National University of Ireland, Galway. Dr Mary Harris, whom I was very fortunate to have as a supervisor, was extraordinarily helpful, patient (especially towards the end) and wise in her guidance. I would also like to thank my wife Céline, whose task of proofreading was not made any easier by virtue of the fact that military history is not her primary interest.

Appreciation and thanks are extended to Commandants Liam Campbell and Victor Laing and the staff of the Military Archives at Cathal Brugha Barracks, Rathmines, Dublin, for their generous assistance, encouragement and hospitality and especially for the reproduction of Witness Statements from the Bureau of Military History. Thanks are extended to Mr Austin Vaughan and Mr Ivor Hamrock of Castlebar Library; their courtesy and assistance is greatly appreciated. Thanks also to Mr Stuart Eastwood of The Border and King's Own Royal Border Regiment Museum at Carlisle. His ready assistance was invaluable. Mr Anthony Richards of the

Imperial War Museum, London was extremely helpful and appreciation for the professional help and courtesy of his staff must be recorded. Major Pete Cottrell, AGC (ETS), British Army and Mr Peter McGoldrick from Liverpool are very much thanked for their valuable advice, sources and general material provided. Mr David Truesdale, military historian, author and friend is thanked for his encouragement and advice. I also want to extend my thanks to Ms Claudia Friese, Boston, USA, for her invaluable assistance.

I want to extend a special thanks to Mr Tomás and Mrs Joan Ó hÉanacháin, both retired teachers and historians in Tourmakeady for their time and hospitality. Also to Mr Tomás O'Toole of 'O'Toole's' (formerly 'Hewitt's Hotel') in Tourmakeady whose valuable information on local history was very much appreciated.

Glossary of Military Terms

Adjutant	Officer who advises the Commanding Officer on personnel matters.
An tÓglach	IRA journal of the period (The Volunteer).
Auxiliaries	A counter terrorist force composed of ex-military officers, independent of the RIC. Official title Auxiliary Division RIC, ADRIC.
Battalion	A unit of 500 plus men commanded by a Lieutenant Colonel.
2 Battalion	Second Battalion of a regiment.
Black and Tans	Ex-soldiers recruited to bolster the RIC.
Border Regiment	Regiment recruited from the English/Scottish border area.
2 Borders	Second Battalion of the Border Regiment.
Brigade	Formation with a number of Regiments and support units.
Brigadier/ Brigadier General	Commander of a Brigade.

Buckshot	A type of shot for a shotgun cartridge, often homemade in the period.
Captain	Officer second in command of a Company.
Carbine	Shorter version of a standard rifle.
Cartridge	Container with propellant and bullet/shot for use with small arms.
Colonel	Commander of a regiment.
Commandant	IRA rank of the period commanding a Battalion or Brigade.
Company	Sub unit of a Battalion. 120-plus strong normally commanded by a Major.
Company Commander	Officer commanding a company.
Crossley Tender	Ex-RAF ground crew vehicle adapted for use in Ireland. It carried a Section of men seated in the centre back to back facing outwards for observation and rapid exit.
Cumann na mBan	Women's Republican movement.
Dennis 3-Ton Lorry	British Army lorry carrying up to twenty-five soldiers.
Division	Formation commanded by a Lt Gen containing a number of Brigades.
Drive	Cordon and Search. The term 'drive' derived from hunting parlance. This

	type of operation was developed in the Boer War.
DSO	Distinguished Service Order (Gallantry award).
Flying Column	IRA combat team of Platoon – Company strength belonging to a Brigade.
Galway Brigade	British Army Brigade, (HQ Galway and incorporated Counties Galway and Mayo) of 5 Division commanded by Colonel Chaplain DSO. It was unusual to have a Brigade so titled, i.e. without a numeral. There were two such examples, Kerry and Galway. These were temporary Brigade type formations commanded by Colonels, not by Brigadier Generals as was normal.
GOC	General Officer Commanding. An officer of General rank commanding a formation, i.e. Brigade, Division etc.
Head Constable	RIC rank senior to sergeant.
Intelligence Officer	Officer whose job it was to collect, collate and advise his CO on intelligence matters.
Irish Guards	Regiment in the Brigade of Guards raised in 1900 by Queen Victoria in honour of the bravery of Irish troops in the Boer War.
IRA	Irish Republican Army.

Irish Volunteers	Antecedent to IRA. See National Volunteers.
ITGWU	Irish Transport and General Workers Union.
Lewis gun	Originally a US design, many countries adopted this machinegun. The British version fired a .303 round.
Lt	Lieutenant, officer commanding a Platoon.
2nd Lt	Second Lieutenant, junior Lt commanding a Platoon.
Lt Col	Rank between Major and Colonel. Commands a Battalion.
Lt Gen	One rank junior to General. Commands a Division.
Machine Gun Platoon	Platoon armed with medium or heavy machine guns.
MC	Military Cross. British Gallantry award for officers.
National Volunteers	Movement set up to counter the Ulster Volunteer Force, which was established to resist the democratic introduction of Home Rule in 1912. It later split, the Irish Volunteers being formed to object to the National Volunteers support for recruitment to the British Army in First World War.
Platoon	Sub unit of a Company, normally commanded by a Lieutenant.

Platoon Commander	Officer commanding a Platoon.
Regiment	A formation composed of Battalions commanded by a Colonel. A sub formation of a Brigade.
Rifle	Individual weapon of an Infantry soldier.
RIC	Royal Irish Constabulary.
Round	Individual bullet.
Section	Sub division of a Platoon. Normally about ten men commanded by a Corporal.
Signal Platoon	Platoon composed of Morse code operators.
Subaltern	Lt or 2nd-Lt.
Troops	A body of soldiers.
Very Light	An illumination flare fired by a signal pistol manufactured by the Very Company.
Volunteer	A Private soldier of the IRA.

Note: IRA units and formations were informal and did not conform numerically to the British Army organisation. Strengths were much lower and variable and the IRA organisation in a village, for example, might be designated as a Battalion, but its strength may be as low as a Platoon.

Abbreviations of Sources

A.O.H.   Ancient Order of Hibernians - Irish
                  Catholic fraternal organisation.
B.M.H.   Bureau of Military History - A dedi-
                  cated team that operated between 1947
                  and 1957 to collect statements, inter-
                  views, photos etc. of all aspects of the
                  period 1913 – 1921.
C na M   *Cathair na Mart* - Journal of the
                  Westport Historical Society.
Mil. Arch.   Military Archives - Irish Defence
                  Forces Archives, Dublin that holds the
                  files of the Bureau of Military History.
R.M.   Regimental Museum - The Border &
                  King's Own Royal Border Regiment
                  Museum. Containing the files of The
                  Border Regiment, Carlisle, UK.
U.C.D.A.   University College Dublin Archives.
W.S.   Witness Statement. Statement given to
                  the Bureau of Military History.

Foreword

On 3 May 1921, the South Mayo Brigade Flying Column carried out an ambush in Tourmakeady, County Mayo in which
a number of Black and Tans and RIC men were killed and
others injured. Following the ambush, the Column retreated
into the Partry Mountains where they later came into contact
with troops from the Border Regiment. This ambush and its
aftermath are significant as the Commander of the South
Mayo Brigade claimed that a similar situation had taken place
to the incident in Crossbarry the previous March when the
West Cork Brigade Flying Column was encircled by vastly
superior British forces. The Commaner claimed that, like at
Crossbarry, his Flying Column had also evaded capture, suffered a small number of casualties and managed to kill and
injure many British soldiers in the process.

By virtue of the fact that County Mayo is the second largest
county in Ireland and had a very strong Nationalist tradition,
it seemed strange that it did not appear to be more promi-
nent in the guerrilla war in comparison to other southern
counties. Many of the actions in the War of Independence
such as the fighting in Dublin, the Kilmichael ambush and
the Crossbarry engagement in County Cork are well known.

A resurgence of interest has been generated in recent years with films such as *Michael Collins* and *The Wind that Shakes the Barley*. However, there were many significant engagements in other counties, which did not achieve or maintain the same prominence and are consequently less well known nowadays. One of these engagements is the ambush at Tourmakeady. This ambush appears to have been an action that was as heroic as Crossbarry and therefore deserves examination, especially as many of the accounts leave many questions unanswered.

In Crossbarry in County Cork, on 19 March 1921, the West Cork Brigade Flying Column, composed of approximately 100 men, commanded by Tom Barry, fought their way through a cordon of around 1,500 British troops and Auxiliaries, inflicting many casualties in this action. Two months later, following an ambush of an RIC/Black and Tan patrol in Tourmakeady, County Mayo, another escape from encircling British troops in the Partry Mountains was reported by the commander of the South Mayo Brigade, Commandant Tom Maguire. The report indicated that there were also many British casualties with little loss to Maguire's Column. The South Mayo Brigade Flying Column had on 3 May 1921, as the Commandant reported, ambushed a police patrol (composed of regular RIC and Black and Tans) in Tourmakeady. This patrol was a resupply detail bringing provisions from Ballinrobe to the isolated Derrypark RIC Barracks, seven miles south of Tourmakeady. A section of the sixty-strong Flying Column opened fire on the lead vehicle, killing and wounding the occupants. The second vehicle's occupants, when attacked, managed to dismount, return fire and manoeuvre their way to Hewitt's Hotel. The ambush and the subsequent firefight lasted between thirty and forty-five minutes. The Column then withdrew, most of the local fighters were disbanded and the remaining thirty or so men moved higher up into the Partry Mountains. A Volunteer called Padraic Feeney was captured by the police patrol at some stage and was later shot dead. Having withdrawn to the Partry Mountains, contact later occurred between the remaining IRA party and British troops.

In studying the Tourmakeady ambush, the immediate problem was with the secondary sources because they are not definitive and are in fact contradictory in many cases. Indeed, some sources contradict themselves, not only in the same publication but in many cases even on the same page. There are a myriad of inaccuracies, which leaves the serious student of events of the period frustrated and dissatisfied. The accounts of these actions vary greatly. Peter Hart's *British Intelligence in Ireland 1920-1921*[1] refers to an intelligence report, which gives an unlikely account, 'The successful round-up of a large body of rebels at Tourmakeady, in which two were killed and thirteen seriously wounded, was the result of an agent's information that the rebels were lying in ambush in this spot.'[2] This quote is an example of fact, fiction and propaganda combined. The only fact contained here is that there was an incident in Tourmakeady and that two IRA men were killed. Thirteen were not seriously wounded and there was no round up of a large body of rebels. The ambush position was not discovered and there was no agent involved who provided information in this regard.

Michael Hopkinson's *The Irish War of Independence* can also be regarded as inaccurate. In the work, the author refers to an attack in the centre of Tourmakeady in which, 'five British

Forces'[3] were wounded. It should be noted that in many sources the use of term 'British Forces' was generic as its use included the RIC, Black and Tans and Auxiliaries, as well as the British Army. The patrol in Tourmakeady was in fact a police patrol, which was composed of regular RIC and Black and Tans. This patrol was attacked and a number of RIC and Black and Tans were killed or wounded. His estimation of the casualties, whether injured or killed is inaccurate, as will be proven later in this book. He also accuses the West Mayo Brigade of arriving too late to help, 'anyone in the ambush.'[4] Considering that the ambush lasted a maximum of forty-five minutes and that help was not and could have been requested, this assertion is not factual. The West Mayo Brigade's Flying Column was later alerted, but this alert and response was to do with the subsequent action in the Partry Mountains that afternoon.

In *Ourselves Alone*, Robert Kee writes of Tourmakeady in County Mayo where another column (in addition to Crossbarry) escaped encirclement.[5] This brief account reflects the basic events, but does not give any information on the ambush, its casualties or the operation on the Partry Mountains, where further casualties occurred and controversy was generated.

Joost Augusteijn's *From Public Defiance to Guerrilla Warfare* refers to Tourmakeady being the South Mayo Column's first action[6] and yet, this is not quite true. The Column did see some action a month before; it involved elements of this Column from Srah, between Ballinrobe and Partry at Kilfall, in which the Company Commander of 'C' Company, 2 Battalion, the Border Regiment, Capt. Chatfield MC was wounded, Cpl

Ball died of wounds and another two soldiers were wounded.[7] This account is therefore somewhat inaccurate.

Martin Mansergh in *The Legacy of History* quotes from Ó Brádaigh's *Dílseacht* and describes a successful ambush against British forces in Tourmakeady in May 1921,[8] in which 'the British suffered ten killed and seven wounded that day with six others being hit.'[9] This clearly is not factual as no British soldiers were involved in the patrol that was ambushed in Tourmakeady and the often-quoted British casualty figures that are alleged to have occurred in the Partry Mountains will be seen to be erroneous. Also making a distinction between being wounded and being hit (as opposed to killed) is quite unique.

In a paper called 'The Tourmakeady Ambush, May 1921' Sean Ó hÓgáin raises even more questions.[10] During the ambush phase he states that the villagers who were taken prisoner were held in the house of Tourmakeady's only Catholic family, the Maloneys. This version of events was taken from an article in the Tourmakeady Parish magazine *Waterfall*.[11] This article was by a John Colleran who was a local teacher in Tourmakeady in the sixties. Colleran translated a talk on the ambush given by Pat Kennedy, a veteran of the ambush, in the school in Easter Week 1966. However, the placing of hostages in the only Catholic house would not have made sense as it would have left them more vulnerable to post-ambush police reprisals.

A contemporary writer, Edward O'Malley, was a Volunteer in 3 Battalion, West Mayo Brigade. He emigrated to the USA after the truce in 1921 and returned to Westport in 1937. He published an account of his life in 1981.[12] In this account, he repeats many of the questionable versions and includes additional inaccuracies when he refers to the actions in the Partry Mountains. He mentions that a British officer armed with a revolver, and possibly wearing armour, was involved, the IRA eliminated sentries in their break out of a cordon, 300 soldiers were involved in the operation and that ten British soldiers were killed and additional numbers were wounded. His description of the British officer's arms and equipment is not realistic and there is no evidence to support the view that sentries were killed and the numbers of soldiers involved is speculative. His estimate of British casualties is just as speculative.

Ernie O'Malley, another contemporary, wrote a series of articles on War of Independence ambushes, which was published in *The Sunday Press* in 1955. These articles were printed in a compilation[13] in 1981 and contain a seventeen-page description of the ambush and after action. However, this account only adds to the lack of clarity already obvious in the aforementioned accounts. It is decidedly unclear why the particular day for the ambush was chosen and how word that the patrol that was to be ambushed was *en route* is also vague. There is reference to a radio transmitter in Derrypark RIC Barracks being used to summon reinforcements, yet this is highly unlikely. Reference is made to policemen accompanying troops on the Partry Mountain following the ambush and this is also questionable.

To date, nobody has published an accurate factual account of the events of 3 and 4 May 1921 or has addressed the inconsistent versions that the published sources contain. In the interests of presenting an accurate account, I propose to outline in detail the ambush in Tourmakeady and the subsequent action in the Partry Mountains. Questions such as what the sequence of events was? What numbers and weapons were involved? What casualties were suffered on either side? What reinforcements were summoned and in what way? I will also explain why various versions of these events emerged, how they emerged and why they had a deliberate spin *vis-à-vis* the intense propaganda war during the period. I will also examine why there was a desire to ensure that certain aspects of the affair would be judged in a benign fashion by history.

Sources I use include statements collected by the Irish Military authorities, British historical and regimental records, contemporary newspapers and periodicals, interviews with military and police historians along with Tourmakeady locals who had contact with or who are related to combatants on both sides and other witnesses.

The following chapters systematically break down the events preceding the ambush, along with examining the actual ambush itself. The final chapters will deal with the aftermath of the Tourmakeady ambush and the reasons for the confusion which surrounds it.

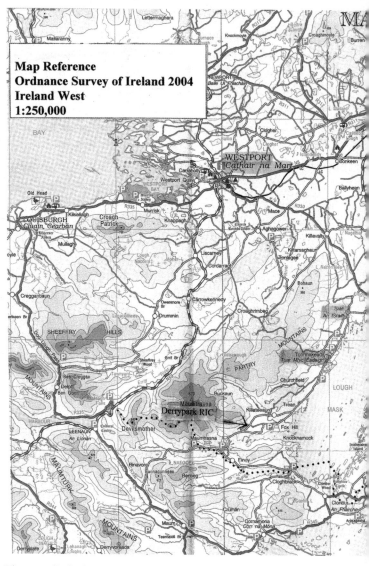

The west of Ireland.

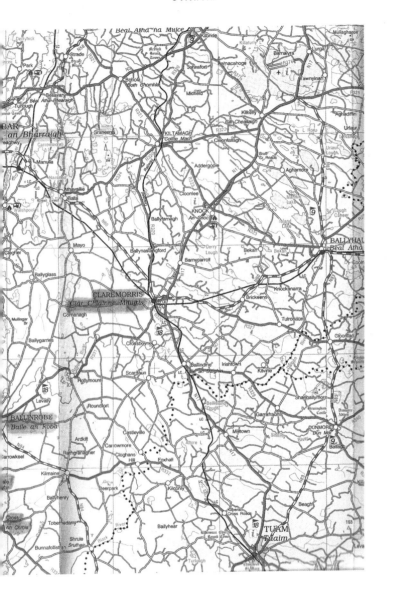

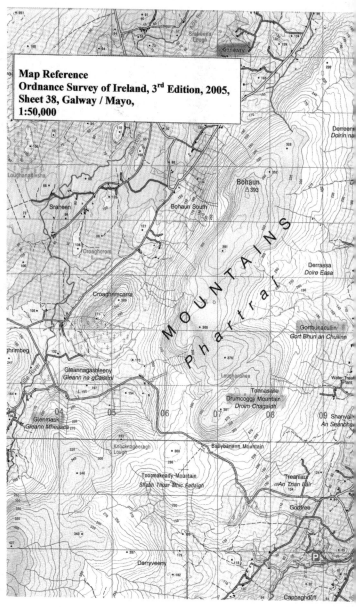

Galway / Mayo.

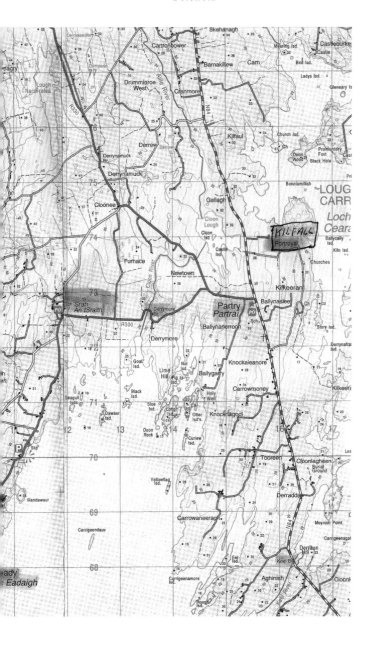

Chapter 1

Background to the Ambush

While examining the background to the ambush, it is
important to look at the nationalist tradition in Mayo
and relations between the community and the RIC in
Tourmakeady. This tradition was tangible and vibrant
in Mayo, as the agitation over the question of land rights
was constant. The county had suffered badly during the
Great Famine from starvation and disease and when crop
failure threatened again in 1879, Straide man Michael Davitt
founded the Land League in Castlebar. The Land League
was designed as an umbrella group to address issues of land
ownership and tenants rights in a campaign that became
known as the Land War. This campaign led to many reforms
being put in place.

Sources that I have used included RIC contemporary reports
and a statement made for the Bureau of Military History by
J.R.W. Goulden.[14] John Goulden was the son of the last RIC
Sergeant to be stationed in Tourmakeady. When Tourmakeady
RIC Barracks was closed in November 1919 Sgt Goulden was
transferred to Ballinrobe. John Goulden, even though he was
only fourteen-years old at the time, took an active interest in
events and often accompanied his father while he patrolled

the Tourmakeady area from Ballinrobe RIC Barracks. In 1956 he wrote an account of the ambush based on his own memories, his father's account, accounts from ambush survivors, the Post Master's account and contemporary newspaper accounts. He is naturally pro-RIC, however; bearing this caveat in mind, his account for the most part would seem to be genuine, if determined to criticise Tom Maguire's (South Mayo Brigade Commander) operation wherever possible. Official military and police pronouncements in the immediate aftermath of the ambush were very inaccurate. The internal reports were better. Records on the Republican side were not without failings. Maguire wrote four accounts of the affair, two in 1921, one in the immediate aftermath and another the following August. A further account appeared in *The Sunday Press* in January 1956 and the last account was given to Uinseann Mac Eoin in *Survivors* in 1980. (See Appendices A,B,C,G). The variation in each account is notable. The numerous secondary source publications perpetuate existing inaccuracies which this book will attempt to put right.

A report in November of 1920 shows thirteen different Nationalist organisations with a multitude of branches and membership. There were seventy Sinn Féin clubs with a total membership of over 11,000, the Irish Volunteers had twenty-eight branches with 66,000 people enrolled, the National Volunteers had thirty-nine branches with over 3,000 members, the GAA had fifteen branches with 876 members, the Town Tenants League had four branches and 169 members, the ITGWU, Cumann na mBan, Ancient Order of Hibernians, Irish National Foresters, Gaelic League and Gaelic Clubs all totalled 771 branches with a total membership of 35,684.[15]

Tourmakeady is a quiet rural village on the shores of Lough Mask in south Mayo. In the decades immediately before and after the Great Famine the area was fraught with contention and indeed, it was a snapshot of the intensity of Protestant landlordism versus the Catholic Irish tenants of nineteenth-century Ireland. Therein, many examples[16] of proselytising, conflict and evictions took place and Tourmakeady became a *cause célèbre* in the international press following widespread evictions in the early 1860s.

In 1905 the village became a leading location in the language revival when the dedicated Coláiste Chonnacht was established and many people came there in order to improve their knowledge of Irish and to learn methods of teaching Irish. Many leading figures in nationalist and language circles donated a subscription towards the funding of the College including Roger Casement, Dr Kuno Meyer, William O'Brien M.P., P.H. Pearse and Major John McBride.[17]

In 1921 every house in the village, except one, was owned by a Protestant and therefore most likely a Loyalist. Mrs Stewart, who was married to an RIC Sergeant, owned the hotel, Tom Whitty, a Protestant steward, lived in the gate lodge near the hotel as did a housekeeper, Maggie Middleton, also a Protestant. The Moloneys, who were Catholics, owned the shop across the bridge and the post office was run by a Willie Billington, a Protestant, who lived there with his recently widowed mother. Further on, on the left there was a vacant house owned by a Miss Louise McDonald of Drimbawn. Drimbawn House was being cared for by a steward and his wife, a Mr and Mrs George Callow. The next house was Tim Robinson's, a Protestant.[18]

Like many other Irish towns and villages there was an RIC

barracks there. It was situated near the bridge, almost opposite the post office. Mr J.R.W. Goulden was the son of the last RIC Sergeant to serve there and in a statement to the Bureau of Military History in 1956 he described life in the village and the changing attitudes before and after the 1916 Rising. The area was crime free and the farmers were getting good prices for their produce because of the Great War. This assessment would appear to be accurate. A perusal of the RIC records of the period shows that while incidents such as intimidation were happening in other areas such as Swinford, Ballina, Westport, Castlebar and Belmullet, the Tourmakeady district was not mentioned.[19] Richard Abbot in *Police Casualties in Ireland*, in his assessment of events shows a similar story[20] with no reported incidents in Tourmakeady.

According to Goulden, attending Coláiste Chonnacht became a symbol of nationalist political views and, while an excellent relationship existed between the RIC and the local people, there was some hostility from visiting students in the summer months. This hostility influenced some of the locals and persuaded them to become anti-Government, especially after 1916.

The pace of life did not change much after the Rising but attitudes hardened after the end of the First World War in 1918. Goulden wrote that,

> The younger men were not really hostile but were to some extent openly defiant, as though unsure how far they could go. They did not seem very clear as to what form this new attitude should take or as to where it should lead them.[21]

This attitude was generally expressed in discussions with Sgt Goulden about the day when the RIC would finally leave. The barracks was like many rural RIC barracks of the period, with no defences other than bars on the downstairs windows. It housed Sgt Goulden, his family and three or four policemen. It was in effect a domestic house that was not defendable against any serious attack. Each policeman was armed with a service carbine and twenty rounds, this was increased to sixty rounds after 1916.

Tourmakeady Barracks was closed on 11 November 1919. This was an unexpected decision and it took both the police and the locals by surprise. The Tourmakeady police were divided between Partry and Derrypark Barracks, with Sgt Goulden's family remaining in Tourmakeady. Life continued

Site of Tourmakeady RIC Barracks on left rear and post office to right rear.

as normal. The relations with the locals continued to be casual and Sgt Goulden was confident that the police were not under any threat. Partry Barracks, among others, closed soon afterwards and the police there were moved to Ballinrobe Barracks. The climate changed in 1920 after Easter Week. Many of the vacated police barracks in the county were burned and the women and children, who had continued to occupy them, were turned out. The Goulden family was left alone but had minor difficulties in, for example, obtaining fresh milk, unless a child was ill. Other than that, they experienced no major problems. Mr Goulden described the change in atmosphere.

> There was always a sort of undercurrent to be felt, but no one was unpleasant though we were frequently asked if we were going away soon. I think the local people did not wish us to be put on the road and just wished to know that we were going.[22]

The Gouldens moved from Tourmakeady to Ballinrobe when a house became available. Three weeks after the move Tourmakeady Barracks was destroyed by fire. Explosives had been used on one of the gables, but without much success.

Many towns in Mayo were garrison towns and British Army units were deployed throughout the county. In 1921 the Border Regiment's 2nd Battalion was stationed in Castlebar, Westport, Ballinrobe and Galway. The Battalion HQ, including the Signal Platoon, and 'A' Company were in Castlebar Barracks with the Machine Gun Platoon at Castlebar Aerodrome. 'D' Company (less 1 Platoon) was in Galway. 'B' Company was in Westport and 'C' Company was in Ballinrobe with 'A' Company's 1 Platoon. Also a company of the Argyll and Sutherland Highlander Regiment was in Claremorris.[23]

The level of experience in the Regiment was impressive. Experience in the post-war British Army was to be expected and 2 Battalion's *Digest of Service* for 1921, showing that it was no exception, cited a sample of officers who were experienced, decorated soldiers. The Company Commander, Captain Chatfield of 'C' Company in Ballinrobe, held a Military Cross, as did the Battalion Intelligence Officer Lt Campbell as well as Lt's Walker and Gronow, while the Adjutant held a Distinguished Service Order and a Military Cross. 2 Battalion was brigaded in late 1920 to the Galway Brigade commanded by Colonel J. G. Chaplin DSO. The Galway Brigade was part of the 5 Division, HQ, The Curragh, commanded by Lt Gen Sir Hugh Jeudwine. The 1 Battalion of the Border Regiment was in India at the time.[24]

The IRA's South Mayo Brigade had companies in Ballinrobe, Cross, Ballyglass and Srah. This Brigade came into existence in 1920 when Mayo was divided into four Brigades. Commandant Tom Maguire commanded the Brigade and the Adjutant was Michael O'Brien. This Brigade initiated ambushes, or had the opportunity to execute ambushes, relatively late in the War of Independence. The Brigade's first action, with a flying column composed of men from the Ballyglass and Srah companies, was at the Kilfall-Port Royal area on 7 March 1921. The Column was commanded by Tom Maguire and included a Martin Conroy from Gortnacoille near Srah, an ex-RIC man, and an ex-Irish Guardsman, Michael Costello from near Srah.[25]

Kilfall is located near Partry, north of Ballinrobe, due east across Lough Mask from Tourmakeady. A Dennis 3-Ton lorry *en route* from Castlebar to Ballinrobe with two officers, Capt. Chatfield MC and Lt Craig, and ten troops from 'C' Company, 2 Battalion, the Border Regiment, on board, was attacked. The ambush party killed one NCO, Cpl Ball (he died of wounds shortly after the attack) and wounded the Captain and two soldiers, Privates Wardle and Southwash.[26] With Capt. Chatfield out of action, the senior subaltern Lt Ibberson took over command of 'C' Company. The next action involving the Border Regiment and the South Mayo Brigade would be near Tourmakeady on the western shore of Lough Mask.[27]

Seven miles south of Tourmakeady there was an RIC Barracks at Derrypark. This barracks, which had been built in the 1880s,[28] was a strong, fortified building and had a garrison of twelve men, both regular RIC and Black and Tans. It was situated in a remote and isolated area, overlooking Lough Mask. Its isolation had been increased in 1921 with the closure of the RIC Barracks at Tourmakeady, Partry, Ballyglass, Cross, Cong and Clonbur. Because of its remote location it was necessary for supplies to be brought by road from Ballinrobe. This situation obviously led to unavoidable routines and therefore security weaknesses being established. Whether a resupply patrol from Ballinrobe came once a month, as claimed by Tom Maguire and brought pay[29] or once a fortnight, as claimed by Mr Goulden and unlikely to have brought pay,[30] provisions had to be escorted on a fairly regular basis. The strength of the patrol varied depending on the account one reads, a motorcar and a Crossley tender or two lorries or two lorries and a touring car,[31] to three lorries.[32] This entailed a journey through

South Mayo Brigade Flying Column.

1. Tom Maguire 2. Martin Flannery 3. -?- 4. -?- 5. Jim Duffy 6. -?- 7. Terry O'Brien 8. John Collins 9. Tom Lally 10. John McGing 11. Tom Cavanagh 12. Séamus Burke 14. Michael Shaughnessy 15. Michael Corliss 15. Michael O'Brien 16. Tom Carney 17. Patrick Gibbons 18. ? Murphy 19. Paddy Maye 20. Michael Costello 21. John Fergusson.

Tourmakeady on the way to and from Derrypark every time, thereby offering an opportunity to an attacker to plan an assault accordingly. Another security weakness on behalf of the resupply patrol was that it purchased the provisions prior to its departure in Birmingham & Co. and other shops in Ballinrobe, thereby flagging its intention of travelling to Derrypark some hours in advance, every time. This routine would have enabled IRA intelligence to pass word of the imminent time and route of the patrol's departure, and type and number of vehicles, to an attacking column. This situation was confirmed by Tom Maguire.[33] He said that an employee in Birmingham's & Co, Patrick Vahey who was a Volunteer, was to let the Column know when the police came to place their order.

Sean Ó hÓgáin describes how the decision on where to attack the resupply patrol was made.

> The route from Ballinrobe to Derrypark was surveyed and a stretch of road with its centrepoint at Tourmakeady Post Office was chosen for the attack…The IRA men in Tourmakeady were to be alerted to the intended time of departure of the convoy by a volunteer in Ballinrobe.[34]

Ó hÓgáin describes how on Saturday night, 30 April, the attacking column assembled at their first rendezvous at the townland of Cahir, just about three miles due west of Ballinrobe. Here weapons were checked and the Column moved a mile north to Cushlough.[35] Here the Column split with eleven men, proceeding by boat to Derrymore Bridge on the Srah/Partry road, about five miles away as the crow flies. The remainder of the column proceeded across country to rejoin at this third rendezvous. They then marched a mile to Srah and were accommodated in houses on the slope behind Srah, which is the eastern flank of the Partry Mountains. The next day, Sunday 1 May, was spent laying low. Monday 2 May, was spent preparing weapons. Both Ó hÓgáin and Ernie O'Malley[36] state that the Column had six men armed with rifles and the remainder armed with shotguns. The quality of much of the shotgun ammunition was questionable. Many cartridges were hand-filled with buckshot, and care had to be taken that these cartridges properly fitted the shotgun barrels. On Tuesday 3 May it was decided to take up an ambush position.[37]

Why this day was chosen is very unclear. The first principle of an ambush is surprise. It made good sense to move the Column near to where an attack was to take place obviously the night before a patrol would arrive. Moving on the day of its arrival, if it was known, would not be practical as it would not have been possible to do this without at least arousing suspicion. Also, it would have been impossible to move to a location, prepare and execute an ambush on a maximum of two hours notice. The patrol would not have moved on the Sunday to resupply Derrypark, as shops did not open so, why not move to the Srah area on the Sunday to prepare for an ambush on the Monday? Spending two days in an area prior to an ambush does not appear to represent a sound tactical decision as the presence of sixty men might well have been detected.

There is no evidence offered to suggest that the patrol might have arrived on the Monday or even the Tuesday. If the patrol had arrived on the Monday, and since the ambush entailed the taking over of the village prior to its arrival, then

Commandant Tom Maguire.

the Column would not have been prepared and the whole operation would have been a waste of time and effort and they would have run the risk of being compromised. The other possible scenario was to ambush the patrol on its return journey. This would have enabled the attacking party to assess the strength and composition of the patrol at first hand and then to move into position quickly, but there is no evidence to suggest that this option was considered.

Maguire attempts to justify the choice of days in an interview with Uinseann Mac Eoin.

> A well-armed relief party went there (Derrypark) on one of the commencing days of the month, but whether it might be the first, second or third I could not say. My intelligence was good but it was not good enough for that.[38]

and:

> It was the beginning of the month....On the Saturday night we came close to Derrypark. We lay low over the Sunday, and on the Monday the 3 of May 1921, we took up positions. We were accompanied now by some local men, but we still had not heard from our source in Ballinrobe. Then as we waited we got the word: they'll be along today.[39]

The passage of years however, may have caused additional confusion. The 3 May 1921 was a Tuesday so he does not explain the decision to spend two days lying low. According to Goulden it was purely by chance that the patrol headed for Derrypark on 3 May. He said that there had been no

Ruins of Derrypark RIC Barracks.

intention of sending a resupply patrol, which was sent every fortnight, to Derrypark on that day. An order had been received in Ballinrobe RIC Barracks on the Tuesday morning to send a Crossley tender, with forty gallons of petrol, that afternoon to Swinford. This, for reasons that are not apparent, meant that the Crossley would not be back in Ballinrobe until the weekend. The only transport available to the RIC in Ballinrobe was a Ford car and a Crossley tender. Sgt Goulden consulted with Head Constable Frawley and decided to send a resupply patrol to Derrypark that morning. By so doing he would have ensured that Derrypark was provisioned and that the Crossley would have complied with the Swinford detail that afternoon or evening. This evidence further confuses Maguire's reasons for the timing of the ambush, and contradicts his intelligence estimate *vis-à-vis* resupply dates and the transport composition of the resupply patrol.

However on Monday 2 May a decision was made. The Column officers 'decided to go into ambush the next morning'.[40] On the morning of Tuesday 3 May, the Column arrived at the Fair Green in Tourmakeady before daybreak. It was expected that the resupply patrol would be composed of three lorries and a touring car, spread out with about 100 yards between each vehicle. This distance between each vehicle would have been in compliance with normal anti-ambush drills and procedures. Ó hÓgáin described the subsequent deployment. The Column was then divided into three Sections of sixteen men each. The first Section, commanded by Paddy May, positioned itself in the shrubbery near the entrance of Drimbawn House. They were on the lake side of the road, behind a double wall with a wood at their back in a position where they could monitor anything approaching from the direction the patrol was expected to arrive from. The second Section, commanded by Michael O'Brien, the Brigade Adjutant, occupied a position north of the village by the Fair Green on the inland side of the road behind a fence on the south side of the Fair Green. Across the road was a double wall, which was expected to be a difficult obstacle to defeat while under fire. Three men were placed inside the wall of the hotel. The remaining Section was placed at the post office with Maguire. The balance of the Column was placed as linkmen between the three Sections.

Each Section was tasked with attacking a patrol vehicle. The plan was for the car (it seemed to be presumed that it would be the lead vehicle) to be allowed through until it reached the Section at Drimbawn House. When it did reach this Section it was hoped that the other two Sections would be in a position to engage the second and third vehicle. It is difficult to understand why no thought was given to blocking the road at the southern end of the target area. If the first vehicle was not disabled, and there was no guarantee that it would have been, then it would have been able to drive out of the killing area and either engage the column or make its escape. Goulden questions the wisdom of the positioning of the Fair Green Section. He reckoned that it gave them a clear field of fire but as they were armed mainly with shotguns, they were at the limit of their effective range. If they had been counter attacked, their avenue of escape would have been over open and rising ground made them easy targets with no cover and in a situation where they had no ability to return effective fire. He also said that if the attack had been made on the return journey, escape for the Column would have been easier as, 'the remaining hours of daylight would have been much fewer and darkness would have helped to cover their retreat or dispersal.'[41]

His assessment here is somewhat flawed as the patrol would have to have spent a considerable amount of time in Derrypark, which was only seven miles away, to return anywhere near dusk in early May because of the amount of daylight in that month. In any case, the patrol had no time to waste that day, as it had to return to complete the Swinford journey.

The local people and visitors (guests in Hewitt's Hotel) were rounded up and kept prisoner early that morning. O'Malley states that people were brought away from the danger zone and placed under guard at an end house. The prisoners included an RIC pensioner and his wife. His wife attempted to escape but was prevented. Ó hÓgáin mentions that the prisoners were held with the Maloneys, the Catholic family that owned the shop. Goulden, however, is adamant that the prisoners were detained in Robinson's house. He explained that the reason would have been that in the event of reprisals by the Crown, it was unlikely that reprisals would have been carried out against Protestants, as they would have been potential enemies of the IRA. This evidence is also reflected in O'Malley's account on his map.[42] Be that as it may, all of the people in the village were taken prisoner and placed under guard. The only exceptions were Mr Robinson and his mother who were kept at the post office. Perhaps this was in order that any incoming calls would be dealt with so as to maintain a semblance of normality, but leaving the communications intact after the Column withdrew seems to be have been a bad tactical decision, if it was a decision.

In Ballinrobe later that morning Sgt Goulden was organising the personnel and vehicles that were to take part in the resupply patrol. The vehicles, a Ford car and a Crossley Tender, Ballinrobe RIC's only vehicles, were prepared. Four RIC men were detailed to travel in the car, Sergeant John Regan, Constables O'Regan (driver), Oakes (Black & Tan), and Flynn. The detail in the Crossley comprised of: Sgt Goulden, Constables Cruise (driver), Power, Morrow, Donaghue, Coghlan (Coughlan), Wright, Clavin and one other. The total party including the drivers consisted of thirteen men. The provisions were gathered at shops in the town and it is thought that they left Ballinrobe between

12p.m and 12.30p.m. Before leaving, Head Constable Frawley changed with Sgt Goulden, as he knew that the Sergeant was busy in the office and he looked forward to the trip, as the day was fine.[43]

The patrol then left Ballinrobe, the Ford in the lead followed by the Crossley at a distance of about 100 yards. The likelihood of an attack would have been in their minds, especially following the attack on the Border Regiment two months previously. Anti-ambush drills and procedures would have been part of the normal briefing and when they arrived at Derrymore Bridge, a likely ambush spot because of sharp corners and a narrow crossing point they dismounted and crossed it tactically. They then remounted and continued

Opposite Drimbawn Gate.

their journey towards Tourmakeady. Travelling towards the village, they would not have expected trouble as it was considered a safe area and nothing unduly concerned them. The question as to exactly how word was received is not well recorded. Tom Maguire told Mac Eoin that while they were in position word came 'they'll be along today'. How and where did this word come? According to Maguire, Patrick Vahey, who worked in Birmingham's & Co. was to be the informant as soon as the police came to place their order.[44] Ernie O'Malley reports:

> When the police in the car and the Crossley tender had drawn up at Birmingham's, Padraig Feeney set out by bicycle to bring this information, but he but he did not reach the Brigadier in time. Another volunteer, Patrick Vahey was able to get through … just ahead of the convoy.[45]

If Feeney set out to inform the Column about the patrol why did he not reach them? Ó hÓgáin states that as Feeney was cycling towards the Column the police convoy must have passed him on the road and he was made a prisoner. So did Feeney leave Ballinrobe after Vahey? It would seem so and it would seem that there was no co-ordination there. Accounts suggest that Vahey left Birmingham's in Ballinrobe having seen the preparations for resupply. Feeney, at a later stage, also went towards Ballinrobe, whether or not he knew that Vahey had also left. O'Malley attempts a further explanation.

> Young Pádraic Feeney, who had tried to bring out word from Ballinrobe saw the military escort pass him on the way. He

was too late to bring the required information but he thought
that he might be permitted to join the men who were ready
to fight.[46]

This contradictory version would imply that he had nothing
to do with getting word to the Column. The implication
is that he left Ballinrobe well after Vahey and that the RIC
(not military) passed him *en route*. This means that he also
would have known that the patrol had been ambushed, as
he would have heard the firing, yet he continued to cycle
into Tourmakeady. O'Malley then says that Feeney arrived
in Tourmakeady after the Column had withdrawn and was
captured by the police and taken to Hewitt's Hotel. He was
then taken by some of the Old RIC out a back door and
shot dead, his dead body being found after the police had left
Tourmakeady. Ó hÓgáin offers a similar explanation for his
capture and death.[47]

Goulden however, offers a different explanation. He agrees
that Feeney was captured after the attack opened and was held
prisoner in the hotel. He also says that Feeney escaped and
ran up towards the rectory gate. A Tan apparently knelt on
the road, fired at him and missed and then killed him with
a second shot. The Tan, who was proud of his marksman-
ship was furious that he had missed him with the first shot
(a distance of less than seventy yards). A bullet hole in the
rectory gateway wall was visible until 2007 when the owners,
tired of curious visitors, filled it in and painted over it.

In an interview with Joan Ó'hEánacháin, wife of Tomás
Ó hEánacháin (both retired teachers and local historians
in Tourmakeady) she stated that Feeney stopped at a cottage between Srah and Tourmakeady and spoke to a woman

who warned him against proceeding any farther as the sound of gunfire was evident.[48] He insisted on continuing into Tourmakeady however, and was duly arrested. In any case Patrick Vahey, who had left before Feeney, arrived in Tourmakeady and warned the Column that the resupply patrol was preparing to depart Ballinrobe and was headed for Derrypark via Tourmakeady.

Memorial to Padraic Feeney.

Chapter 2

Ambush and Evasion. The Nationalist Version.

This chapter concerns itself with the examination of the various versions of events as described by Tom Maguire, his contemporaries and more recent Nationalist writers. Many issues arise therein, not least the discrepancies in the relating of events by the authors, both individually and collectively. These discrepancies will include the timing of events, how the RIC summoned assistance after the ambush, how many policemen and soldiers arrived and how they were deployed. Other issues include, for example, when Maguire's men retreated to the Partry Mountains, how many troops they encountered and how long the action lasted? Were they surrounded and if so did they fight their way out? The question of casualties and weapon losses will also be addressed.

On receipt of the warning that the patrol was *en route*, the Column prepared for action. The Ford car arrived and was allowed to continue for about 400 yards until it reached Drimbawn. The IRA Section there opened fire and the driver was killed. The car crashed into the inturn of the gateway and the three other occupants were thrown on to the road. Further fire was then brought to bear on the three remaining occupants. O'Malley[49] claims that all were then killed and Ó hÓgáin[50] states that six rifles and ammunition were then taken from the car. Maguire stated that three rifles, three revolvers and holsters were captured.[51] However in an interview with Ernie O'Malley he stated that four rifles were taken.[52] There will, however, be evidence that Sgt Regan's rifle and revolver in addition to two other rifles and revolvers were captured.

The Crossley, following approximately 400 yards to the rear of the Ford, then came under fire as it passed through the Fair Green. Constable Power was hit by a rifle bullet and killed, while Constable Morrow was wounded in the arm. Morrow later had his arm amputated.[53] The Crossley pulled up short of Hewitt's Hotel and the policemen quickly got out and returned fire. By a series of fire and manoeuvre, the policemen moved into the hotel area, from where they continued to return fire on O'Brien's Section with rifles and rifle grenades. After a short time the IRA Column broke off the engagement and withdrew from Tourmakeady.

The question of the time of events here is relevant, as it will relate to the alerting and arrival of more police and the military. Ó hÓgáin says that the patrol was expected to arrive about 12p.m. but does not justify this. If, as O'Malley says, that Vahey arrived just ahead of the patrol, then the warning was immediate and it is indicative that patrol did arrive prior to 1p.m. Therefore, if the action lasted half an hour as Maguire suggests, the Column would have withdrawn at about 1.30p.m, 'At about 1 o'clock p.m. the first car (a Ford) was sighted, and this was allowed to proceed to the first party who engaged it, according to plan, the driver being instantly killed and the car running into the ditch.'[54]

The Column withdrew in contact from Tourmakeady at about 1.30p.m. and the alarm was raised. Maguire, while later reporting on the events that unfolded, claims that the alarm was raised by radio: 'I have since learned that they were summoned through a wireless installation in Derrypark Barracks.'[55] O'Malley agrees and also stated that, 'Soon after the IRA had left the village the RIC were able to venture out. They made use of the telegraph in the local post office, but a wireless transmitter in the barracks at Derrypark had already sent information to Ballinrobe about the attack on the convoy.'[56] These reports cannot be seen as feasible. Derrypark is about seven miles from Tourmakeady and the chances of hearing the exchange of fire were extremely unlikely. Even in the unlikely event of the very faint sound of gunfire being heard it would not have been possible to identify where it was coming from or to analyse what was happening.

Maguire then made his way westward into the Partry Mountains and north towards Srah where he dismissed most of the local men involved in the attack retaining a couple to act as guides. The remaining strength numbered about thirty.'Having dismissed half his force, the Republican Officer Commanding retired with thirty men to the neighbouring hills where the column rested.'[57] At this stage they were about two miles above Srah. In Maguire's second report he says that he rested about half an hour and while he rested and he saw activity towards Ballinrobe.

I counted 24 lorries coming towards the scene of the ambush.
… immediately the fight commenced, the lorries coming from

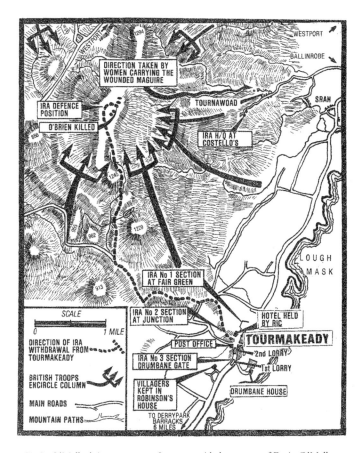

Ernie O'Malley's incorrect map. Image provided courtesy of Ernie O'Malley.

Galway, Claremorris and Ballinrobe. Some of them rushed up
the sides of our SE and SW the remainder remaining south
and opening fire on the hills.[58]

O'Malley also wrote that Maguire saw twenty-four dust
storms.[59] If these lorries were the standard troop transporters,

Dennis 3-ton lorries, then that would have meant that a maximum of 600 troops may have been *en route*. This was also stated in his original report as quoted in Macardle's *The Irish Republic*: 'They reported that the party first sighted consisted of twenty-four lorries of soldiers and that this force had been distributed to the south, south-east and south-west of the Republican position and were advancing on it.'[60] Ó hÓgáin, in his account, writes of twelve lorries on the Partry/Tourmakeady road and like Ernie O'Malley mentioned that Galway, a Brigade Headquarters, and Claremorris had sent troops.[61] However, later in *Survivors*, Maguire estimated a total force of more than 250,[62] which would have taken a minimum of twelve lorries.

In analysing the situation and taking into account that the Column had left an ambush where they were forced to retreat and were additionally nervous, knowing reinforcements had been summoned, it is possible that they over-estimated, or in hindsight, mixed up this figure with troop arrivals later in the day. As for troops arriving from Galway, this is not realistic. Requesting troops from a Brigade Headquarters on the receipt of a call-out that required an amount of troops of less than Company strength would not have been a decision that would have been lightly taken. Even in the unlikely event of a request going to Galway (via the Battalion HQ in Castlebar) and it being acceded to, it would have been impossible to get troops and transport, coordinated with troops from Ballinrobe, in that timescale to such a location. Also, it is difficult to imagine how twenty-four separate 'dust storms' could be distinguished in a convoy of twenty-four lorries, unless of course they were coming one at a time, which is improbable.

Maguire said that while his Column was retreating north-wards following the sighting of the twenty-four lorries, troops rushed up the mountain on three sides, firing as they went. O'Malley described the scene thus.

> Lorries halted at intervals along the lake shore, soldiers and bottle-green police jumped out and were soon slowly making their way up in extended order towards the hills. Some of the lorries passed on to Tourmakeady…. and when they reached the far slopes they would steadily help to encir-cle his Column.[63]

and:

> Around them on the mountain were the British forces together with that old historical tradition of Irish merce-naries who now in their bottle-green uniforms helped to guide the troops and later would identify the prisoners and the dead.[64]

Maguire maintained that he headed north but his route had been blocked by troops who opened fire with Lewis guns and that this happened 'at four o'clock'.[65] O'Malley reckons that this happened at 1p.m. and that the Column 'settled down for a long fight'.[66] Maguire reported that they were bombarded from all sides and were forced to take cover.

> The O.C. ordered his men to take cover, and after consultation with them, decided that the Column, now obviously surrounded by over-

whelming forces, would not surrender on any terms ... The Irish troops
had little ammunition and used it in concentrated fire whenever the
enemy attempted a forward movement.[67]

The enemy made unsuccessful attempts to close in but were
beaten back: 'At this time I was severely wounded, a bullet
passing through my forearm at the elbow point and issuing on
the inside of the arm near the armpit, fracturing the bone.'[68]
A while later, when O'Brien, the Brigade Adjutant, was dressing
his wound, they were called upon to raise their hands up.
They recognised an enemy officer, 'who was divested of his
cap, coat and puttees and carrying a rifle. He was in charge of
eight men but these did not approach as near as he who was
within 20 yards of us and the remaining eight just outside the
hillock.'[69] O'Brien attempted to engage him but was himself
shot, the bullet,

afterwards passing through my back under the right shoulder
blade inflicting a flesh wound. Instantly, one of my troops fired
on the Officer and knocked the rifle out of his hand with a
shotgun ... He is also believed to have been struck by a bullet.
On his eight men seeing him fall they also turned and ran.[70]

Maguire reported that they held the enemy at bay after that
and that the fighting went on for a further six hours. He said the
Column's ammunition was limited and rifle fire was directed at
carefully chosen targets and Lewis gun positions. British soldiers
were prevented from outflanking by the Column's concentrated
fire and suffered more casualties when they attempted to do so.
Edward O'Malley describes this in more romantic language:
'This stand by thirty ill-armed men, untrained in the art of

war, against 300 seasoned troops with experience in the recent war, will go down in history with the brave men who held the Bridge of Athlone against King William's army.'[71]

Piquets were left on the lower slopes, firing Very Lights constantly but they were so defensive that the Column found it easy to filter through them. Maguire found it difficult to estimate British casualties but reckoned that they were considerable as many were killed by their own machine gun fire. He saw, 'two policemen and two soldiers killed and one officer wounded in front of our position as well as six soldiers who were knocked out but cannot say whether dead or wounded.'[72]

He admits in his second statement that the Column suffered one killed, two wounded and eight shotguns captured. Other casualties he mentions were three policemen, one near the Fair Green in Tourmakeady, a second near Kinnury village and the another on the eastern slope of Partry Mountain. As regards the strength of the British military the young officer insisted, 'I have also received definite information that there were 600 enemy troops engaged on the hills that day.'[73] However, in a later interview with Mac Eoin he stated that there were 250 troops and that they withdrew at night time.

> It was dark at last, and we had our first respite. Very Lights shot into the air calling in the troops. We could hear the whistles too as they made their way back to the twenty-four lorries that brought them. What a relief it was. We had possession of the field.[74]

This totally contradicts his previous reports that stated that the 'the Irish party (the Column) succeed in passing through British lines'[75] and, 'at 10.30 the enemy troops were recalled with the exception of a guard who kept firing up Very Lights until the next morning. We managed to make our escape during these few hours, after a tiring day's fighting.'[76]

Ernie O'Malley wrote that the British had left piquets on the lower slopes until daylight but that they were so fearful that, there 'was no difficulty for the Column men moving through them in the dark.'[77] He said that Tom Maguire was carried down the mountain at midnight and rested in a house belonging to the Lally family. At dawn the following morning it was decided not to move him. A doctor named Murphy arrived from Tourmakeady to attend him.

> but he [the doctor] had been unable to bring either bandages or antiseptics for fear of meeting British patrols or picquets on the way... In Lally's he made a rough splint for the injured shoulder and he cut up a hastily emptied flour bag, which served for bandage material.[78]

Later that morning as soldiers came close to Lally's house, women carried him towards the bed of a dried-up mountain stream where he was concealed. That night he was carried down the mountain to another house where he had to remain due to the increasing seriousness of his wounds. The Column men again reported that the British were approaching the house where he lay in bed. As he was again moved Maguire heard an aeroplane, which was directing troop movements. During the day they watched in turn and brought him news as successive parties of troops came in his direction. Tom

Maguire reported that early on the morning of 4 May he attempted to leave the house to which he was carried but was too weak and remained there.

> Very early in the morning two Volunteers arrived. Are you able to move, they asked? ... My legs buckled, I could travel no further. The British were everywhere, searching for stragglers such as myself. Still there was nothing for it but to return to the cottage.[79]

Ellen Kavanagh sent for a doctor (now Ellen Lally aged 104) who dressed his wounds with pieces of wood, some wool and a flour bag. Maguire said he remained there until the Saturday night being carried to a concealed position in the bracken during the day, 'At the same time an aeroplane[80] came in low, so low it would deafen you but it passed on… While I lay like that I could hear the soldiers about me, methodically criss-crossing their steps. I was as near as that, but they did not find me.'[81]

In relation to the reported incident at Kinnury RIC Barracks, Seán Ó hÓgáin wrote that when some of the Section that had ambushed the first vehicle at Drimbawn Gate reached the ground above Srah, a lorry load of troops dismounted on the road below them and began to climb up the mountain on foot. The men from the Section took cover in a stream bed and watched as the soldiers, led by a man in shirt sleeves, passed up the gully to a ridge which they crossed to the west side of the mountain. The men were then led by Michael Costello, the ex-Irish Guardsman to the RIC Barracks where they lay in ambush, hoping to attack the eight policemen stationed there if they emerged. They waited 'until dusk'[82] and then made there way to Ballinrobe-Westport road. If this report is true, then it begs the question as to how an ambush of a police barracks was being considered while up to 600 British soldiers were operating in the area? From there they went across the bogs and fields to Ballintubber, and went on north of Lough Carra until they came to Ballyglass. Two of the group, Pat Kennedy and Eamonn Jennings went on to Newbrook Cross through Robeen and across the Robe river at Robeen Bridge, then on to Clooncastle to the house of an ally.

Another report of action on the mountain was in relation to the capture of two men by some soldiers. Edward O'Malley mentions that two men, Paddy King and Phil Hallinan of Glenmask had been captured.[83] Ernie O'Malley also mentioned this. He stated that they had been found on the morning of 4 May, asleep with their shotguns near Glenmask and were beaten by soldiers in spite of their protestations that they, 'had been searching the heights for foxes which killed the young lambs whenever they found them isolated during the lambing season.'[84] Can a claim that two armed shepherds, hunting foxes, fell asleep on the mountain with all of the alleged activity taking place be taken seriously?

Regarding reinforcements requested by the Column it is unclear how these reinforcements were summoned. O'Malley stated that a message was sent to Michael Kilroy, who commanded the West Mayo Brigade, and was located north of Clew Bay at Lough Feeagh. The message indicated that Maguire's Column was in trouble. Kilroy responded with his men and went cross-country from Newport to Aughagower.

The Westport Column Commander received a similar dispatch. They had come as far as Derrycroff river, which runs below the Partry mountains, when they found that they, too, were not in time to assist the breakout.[85] The call for assistance and the reaction by the West Mayo Brigade and the Westport Battalion was confirmed in statements to the BMH by several participants. Ned Moane, Adjutant of the Westport Battalion described the reaction to the request for assistance.

> That night we marched to Creeragh Hill where we met the Westport section of the column. We all now made our way towards Tourmakeady and on reaching a point a few miles from there we learned that all the men who were engaged in the fight there, had got away. Our information was that the enemy had them surrounded and it was to their relief we were going.[86]

Thomas Ketterick who was Quartermaster of the West Mayo Brigade said that while they were setting an ambush at Brackloon Wood, on the Westport/Leenane road, he received a dispatch to go to Maguire's relief.

> We immediately set out for Partry (the Castlebar column had rejoined us), arriving there in the evening. We called at a house owned by people named Tunny at the foot of the mountain; we were told that our men had got away successfully and that there was no use in our proceeding.[87]

Thomas Hevey, West Mayo Brigade Adjutant, describes the reaction to the dispatch:

So accordingly, on 3/5/21, on a scorching hot May day, we raced across the moor and bog from near Clady towards the Partry Mountains. Before we reached Glenmask, we got word that the engagement was broken off, so we returned to the Westport/Castlebar area near Islandeady.[88]

Tom Maguire, in his second report stated that:

The West Mayo Column sent some of their men to our assistance; hearing from an outside source that the fight was in progress, but the distance did not permit their turning up until well into the night when they found the fight was well over.[89]

In summing up the reports of the events of 3 and 4 May it would appear that there is a general belief from the Nationalist point of view that the Column successfully attacked a police patrol in Tourmakeady, killing some and wounding others with no losses to themselves (other than Feeney) and then withdrew to the Partry Mountains where they encountered an overwhelming number of British troops and police, with such varied figures as 650, 600, 300 and 250 being believed. The Column, who were now about thirty strong, managed to hold this opposing force at bay for six hours during which time Maguire was wounded by Lewis gun fire, O'Brien was killed by an enemy officer and another Volunteer was slightly wounded. On the subject of weapons lost by the Column, no mention is made in Maguire's initial report, however his second report says that he lost eight shotguns. Ó Brádaigh mentions the loss of ten shotguns.[90] It would seem that the Column then managed to escape from their predicament by avoiding British sentries,[91] or by breaking through the cordon,[92] or by eliminating British sentries[93] or by leaving the mountain after the British had withdrawn.[94] Maguire was carried to relative safety and received medical treatment. O'Brien's body was left on the mountain and the remainder of the Column got away by various circuitous routes without encountering any military or police. Regarding British casualties, the figure varies widely. Maguire, as we have seen, found it difficult to estimate but reckoned that many had been killed by their own machine gun fire in addition to the two policemen, two soldiers and one officer as well as the six soldiers who were 'knocked out',[95] plus another policeman at Kinnury and yet another on the eastern slope of the mountain. He also mentioned that after the British officer had been shot 'his eight men seeing him fall they also turned and ran getting caught between their own fire and ours, six of them were seen to fall'.[96] Edward O'Malley wrote that ten of the enemy force were killed and a number wounded, but that 'this figure may have been greater'.[97] Ó Brádaigh mentioned ten killed, seven wounded and six being hit.

These Nationalist views of events with their many discrepancies are interesting. Discrepancies are to be expected, but considerations in historical research should include for example, whether or not the original reports were adjusted to reflect positively on how the Column acquitted itself, and to what extent subsequent authors embellished received accounts without critical analyses. Did the authors of these accounts set out to be deliberately heroic? Maguire's accounts are erratic.

For example in his first report he makes no mention of loss of weapons and in his second report he admits to losing eight shotguns. When it comes to the third report he published in *The Sunday Press*[98] he was again adamant that no weapons were lost. Newspaper accounts (which I will deal with later) of the period were not heroic, however in his 1956 *The Sunday Press* account Maguire was not only heroic about his performance but was vitriolic in his treatment of the British officer (Lt Ibberson) who survived the encounter. In this article he claimed that there were more than twenty-four vehicles and that they were parked 'standing fairly close together extending from Srah Post Office over a distance of three-quarters of a mile of road'.[99] Yet by the time his 1981 interview with Mac Eoin took place he had reduced his estimate of British troop strength to 250.

The heroic but not necessarily accurate Nationalist account was common. This trend was continued in *Saoirse*[100] following the death of Maguire. In the August 1993 edition *Saoirse* gave a three-page spread covering Maguire's life and funeral and lauded him as a hero and the 'last and faithful survivor of last All-Ireland Parliament'.[101] An heroic but inaccurate testimony was given in his funeral mass appreciation on 7 July 1993, delivered by Dr Brian P. Murphy of Glenstal Abbey in which he said, 'In May 1921, despite being badly wounded, he led a successful ambush at Tourmakeady against British troops in the War of Independence.'[102] The events as related by those involved with the Border Regiment and the police are somewhat different.

Chapter 3

RIC and British Army action and reaction

This chapter examines the reaction to the ambush by the police and the military. It examines the relatively minor differences in the accounts of the ambush and how the RIC summoned assistance. It then examines how this request was dealt with, initially by the Ballinrobe RIC who rushed to the scene, and then offers a detailed account as to how troops from the Border Regiment reacted. These accounts are at variance with most Nationalist versions of events. The discrepancy in how the request for assistance was made by the RIC pertains to more important issues such as, how many troops were involved? What casualties occurred? How many weapons were lost and crucially how long the troops were on the ground? This last point is crucial to this study; if troops were on the ground all night how did the Column escape? Was it by combat or by stealth? If all the troops were withdrawn then the Column had no opposition and if this was the case, how credible is the Nationalist version of the event? If the troops were withdrawn why were they and if not, why did they not close in and defeat the Column?

The contents of this chapter are based on what Goulden wrote on the ambush. Other primary sources that deal with what happened after the ambush are the reports of Major Geoffery Ibberson MBE who was the then Lieutenant commanding (acting Company Commander) 'C' Company, 2 Border Regiment in Ballinrobe and who responded to the call-out from the RIC. In 1956 he wrote a paper that included reports he had kept since 1921. Ibberson submitted them to the BMH (also to the Royal Irish Academy and Trinity College Dublin) on Goulden's request. He also wrote an account in the Border Regiment's magazine in September 1956.[103] This was prompted by Nationalist accounts of the Tourmakeady ambush, which appeared in book form[104] and in the Ernie O'Malley accounts in *The Sunday Press*[105] in 1955, which was mentioned in Chapter 2. Information from the British Army side is also based on the private papers of Lt Gen Sir Hugh Jeudwine,[106] GOC 5 Division (HQ Curragh, the Galway Brigade under command) that are kept in the Imperial War Museum in London. While accepting that the accounts on which this chapter is based will not be pro-Nationalist, they will be seen to have been written in a more methodical style.

According to Goulden, the RIC patrol left Ballinrobe between 12p.m. and 12.30p.m. When the Ford was nearing Drimbawn gate a shot was fired from the gate side of the road. This killed O'Regan who was driving, and the car crashed against the inturn of the gate. The three occupants of the car were thrown out on the road by the impact and when they rose they were all cut down by a volley from the opposite side of the road. Const. Oakes was killed at once while Sgt Regan and Const. Flynn were wounded. Elements of the attacking Section then arrived and disarmed the dead. Flynn heard someone say 'You summoned me for a light once, Regan'[107] and then he shot the wounded Sgt Regan who died some time later. Flynn feigned death and suffered no further injury. He made a good recovery and lived in Dublin until the early 1950s.

The Crossley came under fire as it passed by the Fair Green. Constable Power was immediately killed and Constable Morrow was wounded in the arm. The Crossley party returned fire and manoeuvred their way into the hotel area, dislodging the IRA Section in the vicinity at the same time with rifle and rifle grenade fire. As the Column withdrew in contact from Tourmakeady at about 1.30p.m. the alarm was raised by using the telephone in the Tourmakeady Post Office. A phone call was made to Mrs Fitzpatrick in Ballinrobe Post Office, who reported the incident to the RIC. The Ballinrobe Post Office and the RIC Barracks were adjoining buildings. Survivors of the attack obviously checked their dead and wounded first as the telephone call to Ballinrobe referred to Sgt Regan as dying, 'when Mrs. Fitzpatrick tapped the window in the day-room of Ballinrobe RIC Barracks she said Sgt Regan was dying.'[108] This was emphasised by Goulden who said, 'The information was phoned from Tourmakeady Post Office to Ballinrobe Post Office. There was no wireless in Derrypark or in Ballinrobe or even in the military barracks.'[109]

Contrary to reports by Maguire and O'Malley, radio communications did not exist in Derrypark or Ballinrobe. There were some RIC Barracks around the country during the War of Independence, which were equipped with Morse transmitters and receivers. These barracks were in locations where there was an immediate danger of attack such as in West Cork.

In these situations a detachment of signallers, either naval or military, were tasked with operating Morse communications. No such facility existed in Derrypark. In fact no such facility existed in Ballinrobe RIC Barracks or in the military barracks. Radio communications were scarce and only some military barracks in the 5 Division area were equipped with radio facilities. 'By the end of March 1921 there were 60-Watt sets at the Curragh, Athlone, Galway, Claremorris, Castlebar, Boyle and Sligo.'[110]

While this information in itself is not as significant as other discrepancies in Nationalist reports, it does prove that in spite of specific and definite assertions made by Maguire and secondary source writers, the facts are not congruent to those reported by them. According to Goulden, the Ballinrobe RIC then called to the military barracks and reported the incident. Without waiting for the military, every available policeman, a dozen or so, except for Sgt Goulden and two constables, headed for Tourmakeady in locally commandeered motor vehicles. Mrs Regan, the Sergeant's wife and Mrs Flynn, wife of one of the wounded constables, also travelled with the police. This would have meant fourteen people arriving in maybe four cars.

Ibberson confirmed this sequence of events, as he claimed that during lunch in the Officers' Mess in Ballinrobe Barracks, the noise of firing coming from Lough Mask that morning had been mentioned. Then at about 1.45p.m. word arrived at the barracks from the RIC to say that the police patrol had been ambushed at Tourmakeady. Lt Ibberson was the acting Company Commander of 'C' Coy, 2 Battalion, the Border Regiment, whose area of responsibility included

Tourmakeady. 'A' Company, commanded by a Major Munby, had arrived in Ballinrobe Barracks that day from Castlebar, in preparation for a Brigade search operation or 'drive' the following morning, to be conducted against the IRA in the Maamturk area of north Galway. As it was 'C' Company's area of operations and Lt Ibberson was familiar with his area it was decided in consultation with Major Munby that Lt Ibberson should take action with 'C' Company troops.

He made a quick estimate of the situation and reckoned that the most likely route of withdrawal to be taken by the Column was across the Partry Mountains heading west, thereby avoiding Srah to the north and Derrypark to the south. In his preparations Lt Ibberson was able to avail of the following transport, 'Two Crossley Tenders each able to carry nine personnel besides the driver and one 3-ton lorry able to accommodate twenty to twenty-five.'[111]

He stated that two Officers, Lts Smith and Craig were available to travel and that his plan was to send Lt Smith with one Crossley, while he followed with the second and to move through Srah to an area a half a mile south of Tourmakeady. The two parties of troops (one officer and eight NCO's and men each) were then to dismount and to move 300 yards apart and move west, up the Partry Mountain. When at the summit the plan was then to swing around to the right and move northwards to Srah to where Lt Craig and his troops were located. Lt Craig was detailed to move with twenty troops and two Lewis guns to Srah. When he arrived there he was also to move west, up the Partry Mountains, and when he reached Gortbunacullen he was to swing left and to move south until he met up with the other two officers.

While preparations were being made, Lt Ibberson ran to Ballinrobe Post Office and sent telegrams requesting assistance to the Border Regiment HQ in Castlebar and to the RIC in Westport alerting them to the fact that there had been an ambush and that 'C' Company was responding. He requested troops from Castlebar to take the route Castlebar-Killavally-Bohaun-Ravine-Tourmakeady. He requested the Westport RIC to move to Tourmakeady via Winding Valley (see Appendix D). It was normal procedure for those in receipt of information of an IRA attack to react by formulating a plan and putting it into operation.

He explained that the troops left Ballinrobe at approximately 2.30p.m. Their arrival at Tourmakeady was delayed at Srah Bridge when one of the Crossleys had a puncture, however, which was quickly repaired. When they arrived at Tourmakeady, between 3.00p.m. and 3.30p.m., they met the RIC who had left before them and spoke with Capt. Pococke, the District Inspector. Capt. Pococke was unable to say in which direction the Column had left so Lt Ibberson stuck with his original plan. They were later informed that Sgt Regan had died. They carried on past Tourmakeady, dismounted from the transport, ordered the drivers to report back to Capt. Pococke and proceeded to move west towards the mountain. The arrival of this military party meant that with two Crossleys and one Dennis (twenty – twenty-five men) a maximum of seven vehicles had now reached the area with no more than fifty soldiers and RIC men in total. In reaction to the telegram that Lt Ibberson sent to Castlebar requesting reinforcements, a Capt. A.V.H. Wood responded and headed towards the incident with three or four lorry

Early twentieth-century photo of adjoining RIC Bks and Post Office at Ballinrobe.

loads of men. If these lorries were carrying their maximum compliment then it can be assumed that up to 100 men were on board bringing troop strength up to a maximum of 140.

Lt Smith went south about 300 yards before he turned west. Lt Ibberson went through the heavily wooded area of Tourmakeady Lodge estate, to the right of his line of troops and his sergeant to the left. When he emerged from the dense wood only two men, Lance Corporal Bickley and another were still with him. He saw Lt Smith and his troops well ahead of him beginning to climb the slope.

When Lt Ibberson emerged from the dense wood he spotted Lt Smith's patrol a good distance ahead of him. He blew on his whistle to attract the attention of the rest of his men. This action was not successful so he then fired a couple of rifle shots, but to no avail. He waited a while and rather than lose contact with Lt Smith's party he carried on, hoping to spot his sergeant and the remaining troops as they came out of the woods. This did not happen however. Shortly afterwards, he came across a man leading a farm cart. He fired a couple of warning shots to halt and search it. The day was particularly hot so the three men took off their tunics and puttees and hurried on in order to make contact with Lt Smith's patrol. They never did make contact. They afterwards learned that Lt Smith had captured two men and one shotgun in the Winding Valley, 'One was in possession of a shotgun, which had been recently fired. These [men] escorted by a couple of his men, he sent to Tourmakeady. They were tried and sentenced by Field General Court Martial.'[112]

While climbing towards the north they noticed from the crest, a group of four men some armed, about 300 yards to the west. They fired some shots at them and when the intended targets went to ground they quickly followed to where they had seen them. They later noticed the four men again and then a larger group of men which he estimated to number about forty. This body of men was heading towards Gortbunacullen, where Lt Craig and his Lewis guns had been ordered to operate from. The Column then changed direction towards Bohaun so it was necessary to attain a position above its line of advance to force them to again head towards Gortbunacullen. This entailed an urgent sprint to a position six hundred yards ahead of where they were. Lt Ibberson, who was a cross-country runner of note, ordered his two men, who were not as fit, to catch up as fast as they could and headed off on his own.

He reached an advantageous position and fired three or four

rounds at the Column Commander who fell. The Column went to ground and after a while a man broke cover and Lt Ibberson again fired. He realised that the man was going to the aid of the Commander and having done so the man again emerged to recover a weapon, which had been left where Maguire had fallen. Lt Ibberson looked around for the two men who were to catch up on him but they had not arrived. He then noticed three or four men about seven hundred yards south of him and thought that they had fired some shots. A Lewis gun then opened fire from the Gortbunacullen direction and some bullets struck the Column position. After a few bursts from the Lewis gun, Lt Ibberson said, 'I rose, waved my arms, signalled "enemy in sight" with my rifle and shouted, "Is that you Borders?"'[113]

He called that he had the enemy in sight and the firing ceased.[114] After a while, fearing that the Column would escape, he spotted a feature known as the 'Rock of the Sally Trees' and found a firing position to dominate it. He saw Maguire being attended to there. He checked his magazine, found it was empty and loaded it with eight rounds. Intending to bluff the amount of men he had with him he first shot one of the Column (Volunteer Bourke) and then called to his imaginary troops to advance and on the Column to surrender, 'Come on my Borders. Hands up, Surrender.'[115]

Totally surprised again, a few of the IRA raised their hands, however O'Brien who was attending to Maguire quickly fired a shot at him. Lt Ibberson dropped, returned fire and killed O'Brien. He was in turn shot by shotgun fire by one of the Column. He was wounded in both arms and the chest, falling, turned and withdrew down the hill and as he did he, was again shot in the left thigh. This knocked him down and he fell among some Column men who thought they were under fire and being over run. Ibberson got clear and as he made his way down the hill he heard the Lewis gun in action again. Given that he entered the woods at 2.30p.m., it would be realistic to estimate that this incident happened about 4p.m.

As Lt Ibberson made his way down the mountain the Lewis gun opened up again. After about a mile he came to stone walls which were difficult to cross because of his injuries and on a couple of occasions the injured Lieutenant had to make a running jump as his arms were useless. After some time he came to a boreen which ran parallel to the Srah/Tourmakeady road. He spotted Lt Craig's lorry and tried to reach it but very weakened he made for a cottage, which had a horse and jaunting car tethered outside it. After much argument the reluctant farmer was persuaded to bring him to where Lt Craig's truck was parked. The farmer's wife sympathised:

> The old woman, who thought that I was dying, knelt beside me and prayed for my soul to the Virgin. These old folks were in a difficult position. To help me was likely to prove unpopular with Sinn Féin and for me to die on their hands would be equally unpopular with the military. I think it was the old woman who influenced the man to take me.[116]

When he reached the lorry a Sergeant helped him down. As he was being helped down he noticed a Lewis gun in position on the road. This annoyed him as he felt it would have been more useful to have deployed it at Gortbunacullen.

He told the Sergeant to take him to Tourmakeady so that he could report on the enemy's position. The Sergeant, however, fearful for his officer's life, insisted on taking him to barracks, wrapped him in a blanket and drove with all speed. On arrival at Ballinrobe Barracks an old officer friend from the Argyll and Sutherland Highlanders, who had arrived from Claremorris in preparation for the 'drive' the next morning, helped him from the truck. Lt Ibberson was insistent that information detailing the Column's position would be sent to Tourmakeady but the preparations for the following morning's 'drive', due to commence approximately nine hours later, took precedence. 'Some time later, Major Munby, who had arrived from Castlebar came to see me. I was adamant that troops should be sent out to re-enforce Craig. It was however, getting late, and the "drive" interfered.'[117]

He spent the night in his quarters being attended to by a Dr Daly who was concerned by a shot that had lodged near his heart. Archdeacon Traynor also visited him during that night. His batman cared for him during the night and escorted him the following day by train to King George V Hospital (now St Bricin's General Military Hospital) in Dublin.

> There Sir William Taylor, the famous surgeon took charge. A swan slug was removed from my chest and later the ulnar nerve, left arm, was sutured with unusual success for those days. The wound in the left thigh, which had just missed the femoral artery, left no permanent damage nor did the four shots, which passed through the right arm.[118]

The other officers who were on the ground that day returned

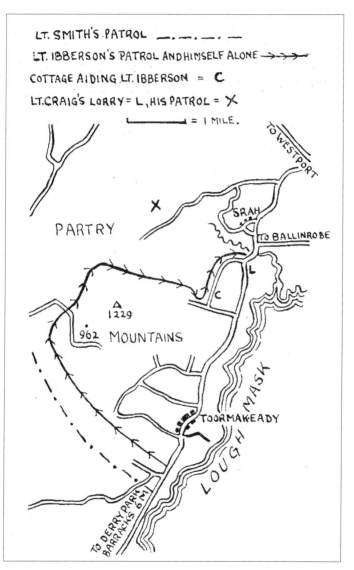

LT. SMITH'S PATROL ― . ― . ― . ―

LT. IBBERSON'S PATROL AND HIMSELF ALONE → → →

COTTAGE AIDING LT. IBBERSON = C

LT. CRAIG'S LORRY = L, HIS PATROL = ✕

⌐――――⌐ = 1 MILE.

TO WESTPORT

SRAH

TO BALLINROBE

PARTRY

L

C

△
1229

962   MOUNTAINS

LOUGH MASK

TOORMAKEADY

TO DERRYPARK
BARRACKS 6 M!

Lt Ibberson's map.

to their barracks before nightfall. According to Ibberson, Lt Smith, who had captured the two men earlier in the day, spent some time searching the area and withdrew to Tourmakeady. Lt Craig, while in the Gortbunacullen area with six soldiers, spotted groups of men running and personally engaged them with a Lewis gun. When he saw the Column he first 'mistook them for RIC'[119] as he was below the Column and facing the sun. He recognised Lt Ibberson's voice, fired at the Column and received fire in return. He then fired Very Lights to attract reinforcements but none arrived. 'He lost contact with the Column and withdrew towards nightfall'. [120] Lt Ibberson explained that the reinforcements from Castlebar Barracks, commanded by Capt. A.V.H. Wood, went, he thinks 'with three or four lorry loads of men to Tourmakeady … there were some RIC with him. From his description he appears to have gone to Derrypark Police'.[121]

Capt. Pococke, having sent the dead and wounded to Ballinrobe, also brought a party to Derrypark.[122] Capt. Wood, commanding the troops from Castlebar, had disregarded the route (climbing over the hills via Bohaun and Ravine) sent by telegram by Lt Ibberson as he was constrained by time. He had orders to be back in Castlebar by 7p.m. so as to rest his troops who, 'would be setting off for the operation in County Galway.'[123]

Another reason that a more aggressive reaction to the call-out was not provided is that call-outs by the RIC were not unusual and another call-out to Tourmakeady the day before an important Brigade operation was not going to alter plans in any way. 'It must be realised that during the preceding months the Battalion had been called on several occasions with little result, the enemy having fled and dispersed.[124]

On 4 May, two search parties went from Ballinrobe, one commanded by Lt Smith and accompanied by Sgt Goulden, the other an RIC party. Lt Smith's party recovered sixteen shotguns. The police party recovered O'Brien's body and an assortment of weapons.

> About 24 assorted weapons, mostly shotguns, but some rifles, were collected from the hillside on 4 May. The rifle and revolver which had been captured in the ambush from the dead Sgt Regan RIC were recovered.[125]

John Goulden confirms the capture of weapons: 'They found O'Brien's body and some twenty-seven guns, and Sgt Regan's rifle and revolver' and 'My father who was a truthful man, told me he got twenty-seven guns...I saw them myself but did not count them.'[126]

So which version of events should be accepted, the Nationalist version or the Army and RIC connected sources? Assertions made by both Maguire and many secondary source writers such as Ernie O'Malley are now proven to be incorrect, for example, the use of a wireless transmitter in Derrypark RIC Barracks. It has also been seen that no policemen were on Partry Mountain on 3 May. Their role was confined to extracting their dead and wounded from Tourmakeady and afterwards visiting Derrypark RIC Barracks. They were not on Partry Mountain with Lt Ibberson's troops on 3 May, they were involved on 4 May in the follow up search, which discovered O'Brien's body, and the weapons the Column lost. Also, and most significantly, it has been seen that in spite of several reports by Tom Maguire that the Column was surrounded by a large number of troops and that the Border Regiment put an overnight cordon in place, these reports were not true.

These reports, some of which were later contradicted by Maguire for example, admitting that all British troops withdrew at nightfall, were the basis for many secondary source writers who wrote stirring accounts of a surrounded Column successfully holding out against overwhelmingly superior numbers on Partry Mountain. It is understood that both the British authorities and the IRA were involved in a major propaganda war and that many reports were greatly exaggerated, leaving the reader of this propaganda with little or no idea as to the actual facts. Therefore it is now necessary to look at the aftermath of the incident and to look at contemporary and other newspaper accounts.

Chapter 4

The Aftermath

This chapter will look at what happened to the dead and will examine the evidence of events as reported in the newspapers. It will also look at the aftermath of the affair, such as what happened to Maguire and Ibberson, and to the gallantry awards issued to the military and police. The evidence of the press will be seen as inaccurate, in many cases, and a lesson in why some newspaper reports might not be used as unsupported evidence when conducting historical research. Exaggeration of events will not be seen to be confined to either side. It is interesting to note that the press coverage was extensive. Apart from coverage in Mayo and Galway papers, the leading national papers and *The Times* of London carried reports on the affair, albeit not editorials. The ambush aftermath was generally reported as being part of the 'drive' that took place on 4 May. This adds to the confusion. The reports generally were dramatic in nature and much space was devoted to the incident in the local papers. The national press was just as bombastic but tied the reports in with other equally dramatic incidents around the country. Many of the false casualty estimates reported on the Column side were as a result of misinformation issued by British Army GHQ in Dublin. The tone of the reports in the press could be described as neutral with references to rebels and volunteers on one side and police, military or crown forces on the other. However, more accurate accounts of the affair emerge when evidence from the Malicious Claims Court is reported.

What happened to the dead?

According to Goulden, he visited the RIC Barracks in Ballinrobe with his mother on the evening of the ambush. The dead RIC men and Tans had been coffined. Reprisal in Ballinrobe was limited and the leader of the Catholic clergy, Monsignor Dalton publicly thanked his father for his part in preventing further damage. Three windows were broken: Newton's, Feeney's and Barnie Joyce's. In Tourmakeady the Co-operative Stores, the empty house near Drimbawn gate, and Tom O'Toole's were destroyed as a reprisal on the night of the ambush. On 4 May Sgt Regan's body was removed by road and Constables Power and O'Regan's bodies were placed in the Catholic Church, as was the body of Padraic Feeney. Constable Oakes was placed in the Protestant Church. All the bodies except Feeney's were taken to the railway station the following morning to be sent to their various destinations. O'Brien's body was taken from the mountain by an army/police search party and was later handed over to his family by the Border Regiment for burial.

Newspaper Reports

There were many newspaper accounts of the events of 3 and 4 May. They are significant as they contain some elements of both truth and fiction. For example, *The Irish Times* contained a paragraph on the ambush and said that following the ambush police, two Lieutenants and men of 2 Border Regiment, were rushed to Tourmakeady reaching the village at about 3p.m. It described how Lt Ibberson managed to gain ground due to his fitness and recorded that, 'the other Lieutenant opened fire with a machine gun on retreating rebels in another direction, and eight men were seen to fall. Owing to the distance from their base and the few in number of the pursuing party, the pursuit was eventually abandoned.'[127]

This article also made reference to Patrick Feeney who had been detained but, 'he took advantage of some confusion and tried to escape. He was pursued for some distance across the country, but being unable to overtake him, his pursuers fired on him and shot him dead.'[128] This account intimates that eight IRA men were shot dead and that Feeney was pursued. These reports are untrue. The *Irish Independent*'s report claimed that the Column consisted of more than double the number of men, 'Some 150 rebels had taken possession of this village at 0930 that morning and had prepared an elaborate ambush for the police.'[129] The remainder of the report was similar to that of *The Irish Times* but in relation to Feeney it added a note, 'The death of Patk. Feeney brings to 75 the number killed in attempts to escape or on failing to obey calls to halt, as alleged by Crown forces.'[130] The *Western People*'s report was unrealistic but was right about the military casualty: 'This car managed to get back to Ballinrobe for assistance. In a short time troops poured into the district and gave chase to the attackers over the hill. Three or four of the fugitives are reported to have been killed while an officer of the Crown forces was wounded in the breast.'[131]

The same article carried a report from British Army General Headquarters in Dublin, which shows deliberate spin being introduced regarding IRA casualties, 'An action ensued during which twelve rebels were either killed or wounded. The body of one rebel was recovered and an armed man with a shotgun was captured. One military officer was seriously wounded.'[132] *The Times* report was reasonably accurate apart from the name of the RIC Sergeant:

> The man [O'Brien] wore a Sam Brown belt and was obviously the leader of the ambushers. The party also found 20 shotguns, three German rifles, one service rifle, two Webley revolvers and ammunition. The service rifle and revolver belonged to Sgt Ryan who was killed in the ambush.[133]

The *Connacht Tribune*'s report had an accurate account of the RIC/Tan casualties but confused the 'drive' with a post Tourmakeady operation:

> Following the ambush at Tourmakeady, Co. Mayo, in which four policemen were killed and two wounded, considerable activity by Crown Forces was displayed in Galway. About 2.30 on Wed morning a troop train with a Red Cross van attached, left Galway for the purpose, it was presumed, of intercepting the members of the IRA who took part in the ambush the previous day and who might be crossing from Tourmakeady to the Connemara Mountains. A short time before the troop train left, a pilot engine was sent out to make sure that the line was clear. Aeroplanes also left Galway and hovered over

the Partry and Connemara Mountains during the morning and afternoon.

Arriving in Recess in the early hours of the morning, the troops detrained. It is stated that in the Recess District a number of young men were rounded-up and kept for a short period for the purpose of pointing out the lie of the district. A search was then carried out, in the mountains around Recess, but apparently none of the Flying Column was found. Those arrested in the round-up were then released, and the military proceeded to Recess, where they again entrained for Galway, where the train arrived at a late hour in the evening.[134]

The same paper also reported on O'Brien's death five days later. 'Killed in the Tourmakeady ambush Michael O'Brien, described as an adjutant in the IRA, was buried at Cong. The remains were handed over by the military to the relatives and the funeral was large and representative.[135] The article also referred to the finding of O'Brien's body and to the retrieval of shotguns, three German rifles and a service rifle and revolver belonging to the dead Constable O'Brien. Its information on the search in Galway was similar to what was reported by the *Connacht Tribune*. *The Mayo News* also carried similar reports on 7 May but was somewhat inaccurate as regards the names of the police who were killed or injured and what vehicles they were travelling in. However, two weeks later it carried the following report, 'The Derrypark police barracks, situated near Ballinrobe, have been vacated and the garrison allocated to Ballinrobe.'[136]

Newspapers reported military activity from Mayo down as far as Clifden and Recess in County Galway and linked it with the Tourmakeady ambush operation adding to the belief that this operation was in response to the ambush. However Lt Ibberson's account explains this several times in his statement by emphasising that all troops in the area were preparing for a major operation against the IRA in County Galway scheduled to take place on 4 May. A detachment of Argyll and Sutherland Highlander troops from Claremorris had arrived in Ballinrobe in preparation for this, as had Major Munby's Company of Borders from Castlebar, before the ambush was known about. Also Capt. Wood's Company who went to Tourmakeady had strict orders to be back in Castlebar Barracks, by 1900 in order to have rested before the Galway 'drive'. When Lt Ibberson was returned wounded to Ballinrobe he pleaded with Major Munby to send troops to Partry Mountain but this request could not be granted because of the 'drive'. This 'drive' was verified by evidence in the personal papers of the commander of 5 Division, Lt Gen Sir Hugh Jeudwine who reported in a paragraph entitled 'Drive of the Maun [*sic*] Turk Mountains, County Galway, May 4th'.

> A Drive of the Maun Turk Mountains was carried out by the Galway Brigade with a view to rounding up a small rebel column ... Detachments from the following units were employed; 17th Lancers, 2nd Bn. The Suffolk Regiment, 2nd Bn. The Border Regiment, and 2nd Bn. Argyll & Sutherland Higherlanders.[137]

Malicious Claims Court Reports

Hard evidence is to be found when one looks at the claims by the injured in the courts. Ballinrobe Court held

Malicious Injury Claims the following November and injury and compensation claims in relation to the Kilfall and Tourmakeady ambushes were heard. It was reported that Pte William Wardle, the Border Regiment claimed £2,000 for injuries received in the Kilfall ambush and was awarded £960 with costs and £27 expenses. Lt Ibberson (described as Lt Emmerson) claimed £5,000 compensation for his injuries and was awarded £6,350 with costs and £68 expenses. Constable Morrow claimed £5,000 compensation for the loss of his arm and was awarded £5,000 with costs and £27 expenses. Constable Flynn (who had feigned death after the Ford car was attacked) was awarded £920 with costs and £20. 13s expenses. Constable Coghlan was awarded £9 for a coat, which was destroyed during the attack.[138]

Mrs Hewitt was awarded £30 with costs and expenses for damage done to her hotel on 3 May. Tourmakeady Co-operative Society was awarded £2,725 with costs and £10. 10s expenses. Mr William Maguire, father of Commandant Tom Maguire, claimed for the destruction of a house he had at Cross and another at Dowagh on 11 May and 13 May respectively and was awarded £600 and £27 expenses. Mr P. J. O'Toole claimed £6,673. 16s. 7d for his premises and stock that were burned by Crown forces and was awarded £6,000 plus costs and expenses. Mrs Woods, who claimed for the destruction of Drimbawn mansion, was awarded £965 with expenses. Mr Richard Feeney, uncle of Patrick Feeney who was shot in Tourmakeady claimed for the destruction of his premises.[139]

Malicious Claims Court evidence on weapons losses

In evidence at the Claims Court when referring to his initial contact when L/Cpl Bickley and the other soldiers were with him Lt Ibberson stated that, 'on top of the mountain he saw a party of four men, armed with what appeared to be shot guns. They came out and he gave his men directions to open fire and the four men dropped what they had and ran away.'[140]

What Happened the Combatants

Comdt Tom Maguire eventually recovered from his injuries. On 19 May 1921 he was elected to the Second Dáil. When the IRA was being reorganised into divisions he was given command of 2 Western Division with the rank of Commandant General. He took the anti-treaty side in the Civil War and was captured and imprisoned by Irish Army troops. He married Christina Feeney, a sister of Padraic Feeney in 1924 and remained a non-constitutional Republican all of his life. He died in 1993 at the age of 101.

Lt Ibberson was so badly wounded that he continued to serve as a Lieutenant in a reserve Battalion of the Border Regiment for many years. He was finally promoted to the rank of Captain[141] in 1929 and was restored[142] to the regular establishment in 1933. He retired as a Major having spent a short time as an acting Lieutenant Colonel. He was married in 1923 to a Mary Dorothea Rochfort Turnly the daughter of Mr F.J.S. Turnly, Lisloughry, Cong, County Mayo[143] (Lord Iveagh's agent for Ashford). Their first son was born[144] while they were in Malta with the Regiment in April 1927. They were divorced in 1931.[145] In 1949 he married a Kathleen Vida McLaren.[146] He had two sons who served in the British Army, Geoffrey Alexander Rochfort Ibberson who served in the Border Regiment and John Michael de Burgh who served in 16/5 Lancers.[147]

Decorations

Lt Ibberson and Lt Craig were both decorated with an MBE[148] for their actions on 3 May 1921. The citation did not reflect the facts:

> At Srah, on 3rd May, 1921, two officers of the Border Regiment, with one non-commissioned officer and five men, were sent to intercept some rebels who had successfully ambushed a party of RIC. They got into touch with the rebels and attacked them. One of the officers got several hundred yards ahead of the party and engaged in a hand-to-hand fight with the rebels. He shot their leader and the remainder of the party put up their hands, whereupon the wounded rebel fired and hit him. The officer was wounded through both arms but his action had so far delayed matters that the party under the other officer were able to get up to the scene of action and account for the remainder of the rebels.[149]

The RIC patrol that was ambushed was also decorated with the Irish Constabulary Medal. The citation, exaggerating events, from a Dublin Castle Report dated 15 Feb 1922 reads as follows:

For pre-eminent valour and bravery on the occasion of an ambush at Tourmakeady, Co. Mayo on 3rd May 1921. A party of 13 police in two motors were ambushed by about 200 well armed men in well entrenched positions. Four men were killed and 3 wounded in the first volley. The remainder, acting with the greatest coolness, left their cars and took cover in a ditch. As the ditch was being enfiladed the police crawled in two parties – one covering the other – to take possession of an empty house. The rebels began to close in and increased the severity of their fire. The police returned the fire and used rifle grenades with such skill that the attackers were driven back and eventually retreated after ¾ of an hour with numerous casualties. The coolness and intelligence shown by the Head Constable and his men were responsible for this favourable result, and probably saved the reinforcements which the rebels expected would be sent.[150]

Three medals were awarded to the patrol in time-honoured fashion, the first to Head Constable Frawley and the second to Constable Clavin and the third to Constable Clews, the driver of the Crossley. The two Constables were chosen by a ballot of the men. This was the tradition in vogue so as to save each individual being awarded the medal. The medal given to Constable Clavin is in the RUC Museum in Northern Ireland.[151]

It has now been shown how the press reports gave an inaccurate account of the events of 3 May, and how the events surrounding the 'drive' on 4 May were confused with the ambush and aftermath. Casualties and weapon losses are more accurately reflected and what the Courts rewarded helps to

Gazette showing MBE's for Lt's Ibberson and Craig.

highlight actual casualties and damage. Citations issued by the British Government to Army Officers and policemen in respect of awards and decorations are seen to contain information that is very inaccurate indeed. In light of this study it can now be seen that citations, which are intended to be 'final summations' of events, should not be relied on in seeking the truth of these matters. This is not a denial of the undoubted bravery of those involved nor that they deserved the decorations awarded, but out of the seventy-four gallantry[152] awards bestowed on British officers and men during the War of Independence, it would be interesting to note how many associated citations reflected accurately the events to which they pertained.

Chapter 5

What Really Happened

This chapter will analyse the ambush and aftermath and critically examine the actions of the participants. The IRA's intelligence estimate judged that the resupply patrol happened on one of the first three days of each month. Mr Goulden states that it was a fortnightly affair, due to happen on the week in question but not on the Monday or Tuesday.

The Swinford petrol supply detail changed this. A resupply every fortnight is more credible as there were twelve men, in an isolated barracks, in a hostile community who would not have been able to obtain fresh food themselves. Therefore the decision to attack on 3 May would seem to have been a remarkable coincidence indeed. No evidence to justify

Constable Clavin's Irish Constabulary Medal (RUC Museum, Belfast).

the Column's decision to prepare for the ambush on that day has appeared.

The ambush was a partial success. Four men were killed and two were wounded with no casualties to the Column. It had potential flaws. Not preparing roadblocks to prevent the Ford from breaking through, had the first volley been unsuccessful, was a dubious decision as was the lack of a similar preparation to prevent the Crossley from turning about at the Fair Green. The plan was optimistic as the majority had never been in action before and the Column only had six rifles with less than fifty shotguns. Many of the shotguns would have been of dubious value had a concerted counter attack been mounted. As it was, the resistance offered by the occupants of the Crossley forced the Column to break contact. The initial euphoria of a successful attack must have rapidly turned into serious concern for their own lives. The lack of action in preventing the RIC from phoning for reinforcements was a mistake. While the Postmaster was kept *in situ* to maintain an appearance of normality, proper planning would have ensured that the disabling of the communications was a priority.

The RIC/Tan casualties were as follows:

Sgt John Regan	Died of wounds	Ford
Constable O'Regan	Killed in action	Ford
Constable Oakes, Black & Tan	Killed in action	Ford
Constable Flynn	Wounded in action	Ford
Constable Power	Killed in action	Crossley Tender
Constable Morrow	Wounded in action arm amputated	Crossley Tender

The actions of Feeney were rash. He may not have known that Vahey had already left to bring word to the Column. Neither man could have known that the resupply was going to happen until the police began to purchase provisions. Youthful exuberance may have caused him to hasten to Tourmakeady. One would presume that the Column had broken contact by the time he reached Tourmakeady, although he would have heard the firing as he made his way there. When he arrived he was taken prisoner by policemen who, after their recent experience, would not have inclined them to treat him with kid gloves. How genuine his attempted escape was, we will never know. He was making a run for it when he was shot.

As regards the performance of the RIC, they appeared to act as a trained body with well-drilled procedures kicking into action. The second vehicle's occupants were well led by the Head Constable. Head Constable Frawley got his men to a position of safety where they fought a defensive action until the Column withdrew. The RIC in Ballinrobe, on hearing about the ambush, moved quickly to commandeer vehicles and go to the aid of their comrades, informing the military as they left.

The Column made their way to the Partry Mountain. Their good fortune in conducting a successful attack was tempered with the knowledge that it had been a close-run thing and that they were now the hunted party. The dismissed local men lost no time in making their way out of the area leaving the thirty remaining men to consider their options. A short time elapsed before the RIC from Ballinrobe and the two police wives rushed to the scene. Their priority was to go to the aid of their men, not an offensive patrol. When they arrived at Tourmakeady, they must have been severely traumatised. They were still at the scene when the Border Regiment troops arrived from Ballinrobe and had no knowledge of the direction to which the Column withdrew.

The Column, making their way up the mountain, would have seen the police rushing to the scene and would have counted three or four vehicles. They then would have seen Lt Ibberson's transport, the two Crossleys and the Dennis making its way and deploying at Srah, Tourmakeady and South of Tourmakeady. Shortly afterwards they may have seen the two Crossleys returning to Tourmakeady when the drivers were told to report to Capt. Pococke. In addition to this they would have seen military transport, again 3 or 4 lorries as well as the RIC transport arriving from Castlebar and Westport. These vehicles drove through Tourmakeady and on to Derrypark to see if any action had taken place there. Therefore the Column, who at this stage may have thought that they saw sixteen or seventeen vehicles, may also have imagined that a considerable force of military and RIC had arrived.

In his first two reports Maguire made reference to troops approaching from four different directions. He saw Lt Craig and Lt Ibberson's parties deploying and making their way up the mountain. He may have thought the Castlebar and Westport reinforcements commenced the climb from the southwest. As regards soldiers opening fire on the hills, there was indeed gunfire. When Lt Ibberson exited the woods he fired some rifle shots to attract the attention of the soldiers making their way through the heavy wood. He then fired warning shots at the farmer who was leading a cart. A short time later he, Lt/Cpl Bickley and the other soldier fired a number of shots at a group of four men. He fired more shots when he engaged and shot Comdt Maguire and shortly after that Lt Craig's Lewis gun opened up. Maguire greatly overestimated the number of troops involved and assumed that they were in fact on the mountain advancing towards him. Maguire in his Mac Eoin interview, while in error about the time and exaggerating the situation said that, 'it was not long until the chase was on. A few hours later at about twelve o'clock, we were contacted by a party of British troops. A running fight ensued. We withstood their attack with Lewis guns and rifle fire all day.'[153]

When Lt Ibberson heard the Lewis gun opening up he signalled to where the fire was coming from and, calling out, asked were the firers Borders. Shortly afterwards, immediately after he shot Bourke and before O'Brien fired at him, he again called out to his imaginary troops saying, 'Come my Borders; hands up, surrender.'[154] This would have sent a clear message to the Column that in fact he had troops with him. A few seconds later when O'Brien's shot missed Ibberson, Ibberson shot O'Brien and was in turn shot by shotgun men. The imaginary Borders did not only not return fire, but obviously did not appear in any shape or form. This may have left the impression that they had turned tail and fled.

According to Lt Ibberson, his and Lt Smith's troops withdrew as already described. Lt Craig opened fire on the Column with a Lewis gun and fire was returned. He then fired Very Lights to attract reinforcements, which did not materialise. He withdrew towards nightfall and returned to Ballinrobe. However, this does explain Maguire's reports of Very Lights being used.

The IRA casualties were as follows:

Michael O'Brien,
    South Mayo Brigade Adjutant.   Killed in action
Tom Maguire, Brigade Commander. Wounded in action
Volunteer Bourke   Wounded in action
Padraic Feeney
    (not part of the Column)   Killed while escaping

Lt Ibberson personally shot all of the IRA casualties, with the exception of Feeney who, as we have seen, was shot by a Black and Tan. The only Border Regiment casualty was Lt Ibberson. What weapons were used and what weapons were captured? When the first vehicle was attacked six weapons were taken with Sgt Regan's rifle and revolver being later recovered. Therefore the police lost two rifles and two revolvers, while the Border Regiment lost one rifle. Lt Ibberson's rifle was captured by the Column and still exists 'somewhere in Mayo' to this day. The Column lost between twenty-four and twenty-seven weapons.

In conclusion, following the shooting of Ibberson, there was no more offensive action by the Border Regiment and they had fully withdrawn by nightfall as there was no night-time cordon. The Column then made their way from Partry Mountain leaving most of their weapons behind along with O'Brien's dead body.

Most of the troops involved in the action were active again in the 'drive' into the Maamturks the following morning. A party searched the area that morning and recovered many of the Column's weapons. The 'drive' itself was not connected with the ambush. There is much local talk to this day about troops from the Border Regiment searching the Tourmakeady/Partry mountain area in the days following the 'drive'. This follow-up search of course happened and it was prolonged. However, while the mountain was searched successfully for weapons and dead on 4 May, the follow-up search could have occured before 5 May due to the fact that troops involved in the 'drive' would had to have been rested prior to commencing another major search.

Chapter 6

Conclusion

The first conclusion that one comes to is that the Tourmakeady story is one that has been laden with misinformation. Much of this confusion has been added to by those who were familiar with the numerous accounts available but failed to take reality into consideration. The whole affair was an extraordinary series of coincidences starting with the matter of the selection of the ambush day.

It must be understood that during the War of Independence, the propaganda war and the rumour machine were considerable forces. Each side lost no opportunity in exaggerating and upping the ante in order to create confusion in the other. D.V. Duff, who was a Black-and-Tan stationed in Galway among other places in 1921, wrote about the rumours and the negative effect that they had on the combatants. Following the West Mayo IRA Brigade's ambush at Carrowkennedy a month after Tourmakeady, on 2 June, 'there were ugly rumours abroad that the "Shinners" had beaten the brains out of the wounded with tools they seized from the lorries.'[155]

Was there deliberate obfuscation rather than exaggeration of the facts by Tom Maguire? It would appear that the former was in fact the case. Again it is important to remember that the propaganda elements of the war were very powerful weapons employed by all participants. The Dublin Castle and Irish Command HQ statements on the Tourmakeady incident were examples of naked obfuscation, deliberately publishing reports that bore very little similarity with the truth. D. V. Duff complained:

> When has there ever been a more fatuous, childish and lying a government publication than the Weekly Summary, a paper issued to us by the authorities and which we were supposed to read? In its pages every 'Shinner' was depicted as a dangerous criminal, as something worse than a thief, false news was also given by it and its methods of attempting to rouse our blood were laughable had they not been so dangerous.[156]

and:

> Then there was the shameful 'Shinner' propaganda, by which we Black-and-Tans were depicted as a dangerous, sadistic, savage band of ex-convicts specially released from Dartmoor to fight in Ireland.

Tom Maguire and his men probably thought that greater numbers were attacking the Column. In addition to this, their psychological state in being hunted and not in a position to expect much mercy heightened their sense of imagination and fear. They had lost their Adjutant, their Commander was severely injured and another was wounded. For most of them it was their first taste of action and being on the receiving end of an attack and under fire from a machine gun was unnerving. The fact that they left their dead and most of their weapons on the mountain must have impinged on their conscience and this would have led to exaggeration.

However did they succeed in their mission? Their primary mission was to attack an RIC patrol and their secondary mission was to cause the closure of Derrypark RIC Barracks. They succeeded in both. Derrypark Barracks was closed on 5 May 1921. However, another result of this ambush was that a company of Auxiliaries was posted to Westport from Boyle later that month. Had the truce not come into effect, who knows how they would have faired? Ibberson takes comfort in the fact that this Column never fired a shot in anger again, but nobody knows what would have happened had the truce not intervened on 11 July

For the historian there is much to be learned from the writing of this book, due to the many pitfalls. In most cases the sources were misleading. The primary sources from the Nationalist side were inconsistent as were many from the military and police authorities. Newspaper accounts varied in reliability, extending as far as court reporting only, in most cases. The secondary sources were even more misleading with many accounts embellishing previous inaccurate accounts. From a military point of view, the examination of the tactical evidence provided showed how flawed the operation was from the start. The fact that the ambush succeeded was more to do with luck and coincidence rather than detailed planning and preparation. Also, the fact that there were not many more casualties on the Partry Mountain was due to pre-planned circumstances and had more troops been available for a longer time, the story may have had a much different outcome.

Had Lt Ibberson decided to start the chase without firstly entering the woods south of Tourmakeady, the outcome would probably have been swifter and more decisive. What was surprising was the exaggeration of events that were published on citations associated with the MBE's and the Constabulary Medals awards. This presents a challenge for historians. It would have been a reasonable assumption that if when a historian was to research the deeds of a recipient of a bravery or gallantry award, the research might begin with the testimony of bravery or gallantry. The historian, impressed enough with this, might then be tempted to work backwards and to discover the story behind the award. Given the fact that there were seventy-four military gallantry awards bestowed by Britain on her soldiers during the War of Independence, and that the RIC were also in receipt of a significant number of awards, it would be interesting, in the light of the findings presented here, to discover to what extent the citations for these awards reflected the actual happenings.

To conclude, in terms of historiography, the South Mayo Brigade rose when they were required to, they sought action and found it, they inflicted more casualties than they received and they earned their place in history through the ambush at Tourmakeady. However, the affair involving contact with troops from the Border Regiment was not the heroic incident that most Nationalist writers indicate and more importantly, it cannot, under any circumstances, be described as another Crossbarry.

Appendices

Appendix A – Maguire's First Report.

Macardle, D., *The Irish Republic* (Irish Press Ltd: Dublin, 1951) p.440.

The character of the fighting in the west is illustrated by the following account – the official Republican report – of an engagement which took place in May:

> At Tourmakeady, County Mayo, on May 3rd, a party of sixty officers and men of the South Mayo Brigade, IRA, engaged an enemy patrol travelling in two motor lorries. After an action lasting thirty minutes four of the enemy were killed and four wounded, one mortally. The remainder of the patrol took refuge in a neighbouring hotel, and the Republicans, after an unsuccessful effort to dislodge them, withdrew. Having dismissed half his force, The Republican Officer Commanding retired with thirty men to the neighbouring hills where the column rested. An hour later the outposts reported the advance of large parties of British troops. It was then about 2.30 p.m. when Scouts were sent out to ascertain the enemy's numbers. They reported that the party, first sighted, consisted of twenty-four lorries of soldiers and that this force had been distributed to the South, South-East and South-West of the Republican position. Acting on the information, the Officer Commanding ordered a retreat towards the North. Using natural cover to great advantage, the Republican forces had traversed a distance of four or five miles when their advance-guard sighted a large party of British troops holding the line of their retreat. The British immediately opened fire with Lewis guns. It was then, 4 p.m. – six hours before nightfall. The O.C. ordered his men to take cover, and after consultation with them, decided that the column,

though now obviously surrounded by overwhelming forces, would not surrender on any terms.

The British forces kept up a continuous fire on Republican positions, which was replied to only at long intervals. The Irish troops had little ammunition and used it in concentrated fire whenever the enemy attempted a forward movement. These tactics had the desired affect. For six hours the exchange of fire continued, but the enemy never attempted to close in. When darkness came the Republican forces decided to break through the cordon, which at nightfall was greatly weakened by the withdrawal of the main body of British troops. Although Very lights were thrown up frequently by the remaining troops, the Irish party succeeded in passing through British lines and escaping, carrying with them two of their number who were wounded. The total Republican casualties in these actions were one killed, two wounded and two captured. Enemy casualties in the fight on the hills as observed by the Officer Commanding were one officer and one constable killed, and one officer and two soldiers wounded It is believed the enemy suffered many other casualties. A short time after the Republican column had broken through the enemy's position two flying columns of the West Mayo Brigade, IRA, arrived in the district. They had come many miles by forced marches in order to relieve the invested columns. Their assistance was, however, not needed.

Appendix B – Maguire's Second report

Maguire, T., 'The Battle of Tourmakeady', *An tÓglach*, GHQ IRA 19 August 1921.

The following is a detailed account of the fight at Tourmakeady on 3 May from the O.C. of the South Mayo Brigade:

Having previously observed that the enemy carried the monthly pay to Derrypark Police Station on the 3rd of each month, I decided to intercept them at a point between Ballinrobe and that station known as Tourmakeady. On May 3rd I arrived there in the early morning with 60 troops under my command, and having previously inspected the ground and having decided on the best points I placed my men in three positions – as I expected three lorries – with about 200 yards between each position. At about 1 o'clock p.m. the first car (a Ford) was sighted, and this was allowed to proceed to the first party who engaged it, according to plan, the driver being instantly killed and the car running into the ditch. After a short sharp engagement the remaining three were also shot dead. Three rifles, three revolvers and holsters etc. were captured.

By this time the other car (a Crossley) containing 10 or 12 enemy was half way between the other two positions when it pulled up. The two parties engaged them and the enemy got out and took cover and a fight lasting for a half an hour ensued. In this battle my troops were at a great disadvantage as the enemy used rifle grenades, mainly, and rifle, whereas my party had but a few rifles and the remainder shotguns and the distance for the latter was too great. Seeing there was no chance of dislodging them after half an hour and fearing enemy reinforcements might arrive I ordered my men to retreat to the hills which was done successfully, my troops having suffered no casualties.

In this fight the enemy suffered heavily. After getting on to the hills, I dismissed the men who lived in the locality and ordered the remaining numbering 30 to rest, as they were a bit fatigued. After resting about half an hour, the scouts reported activity towards Ballinrobe and on training my glasses in that direction I counted 24 lorries coming towards the scene of the ambush. I have since learned that they were summoned through a wireless installation in Derrypark Barracks immediately the fight commenced, the lorries coming from Galway, Claremorris and Ballinrobe. Some of them rushed up the sides of our SE and SW the remainder remaining South and opening fire on the hills.

My party retreated North for a distance, only to find the way barred by enemy troops from Castlebar and Westport, who on sighting us opened fire with Lewis guns and rifles. This again forced us back I then picked the best cover available and ordered my men to get down. The enemy fire was now most intense. We were bombarded from all sides. Under the great strain the troops were quite cool, each man being determined to make the best use possible of his diminished supply of ammunition and the cry was "No Surrender".

It was now about 4 o'clock and the enemy made a few futile efforts to close in on us but we beat them back. At this time I was severely wounded, a bullet passing through my forearm at the elbow point and issuing on the inside of the arm near the armpit, fracturing the bone. The Brigade Adjutant crept up to dress me and slit open my sleeve when a voice behind us called "Hands up". On turning round we recognised an enemy officer, who was divested of his cap, coat and puttees and carrying a rifle. He was in charge of eight men but these did not approach as near as he who was within 20 yards of us and the remaining eight just outside the hillock. The Adjt picked up his rifle to engage him, but the other had the advantage and shot him dead through the body, the bullet afterwards passing through my back under the right shoulder blade inflicting a flesh wound. Instantly, one of my troops fired on the Officer and knocked the rifle out of his hand with a shotgun and gave him the contents of the second barrel in the stomach, 10 grains of buckshot since removed from it. He is also believed to have been struck by a bullet. On his eight men seeing him fall they also turned and ran getting caught between their own fire and ours, six of them were seen to fall.

We managed to hold them at bay after this, my troops fighting like demons, and the enemy seemed to loose his temper as he kept pouring a constant stream of lead for perhaps half an hour without ceasing. In this way the fight went on until the night fell when at 10.30 the enemy troops were recalled with the exception of a guard who kept firing up Very lights until the next morning. We managed to make our escape during these few hours, after a tiring day's fighting.

Appendix C – Maguire's Third report.

Mac Eoin, U., *Survivors* (Argenta Publications: Dublin, 1980).

One of our biggest operations after that was the ambush near Tourmakeady. The British had built a very strong barracks in a very commanding position at a place called Derrypark. We had not the explosives to attack it, and in any case, it would have been a big undertaking to do so. So after the smaller barracks in this area had been cleared, Cross, Cong, Clonbur, it was still left, a thorn in our side, in an area we badly wanted cleared.

There was one weakness in its situation however. It had to be supplied every month. A well-armed relief party went there on one of the commencing days of the month, but whether it might be the first, second or third I could not say. My intelligence was good but it was not good enough for that. However, they bought their supplies in a shop in Ballinrobe, Birmingham & Co., and in that shop worked a boy named Patrick Vahey, who in later years would have been an uncle of Frank Stagg who died – many say he was killed – suffering intolerable conditions in British prisons in February 1976. Anyway this boy was one of our volunteers. When the police came to place their order he was to let us know.

Ever since Kilfall we were on our keeping, a flying column of around thirty men out in the open country sleeping where we could and when we could. The local units in each village were in an important back-up position, not, seemingly doing much, but contributing much in the way of supplies, intelligence, safe houses and of course impeding the enemy at every hand's turn.

It was the beginning of the month. We therefore decided to move. On the Saturday night we came close to Derrypark. We lay low over the Sunday, and on the Monday the 3rd of May 1921, we took up positions. We were accompanied now by some local men, but we still had not heard from our source in Ballinrobe. Then as, we waited, we got the word: they'll be along today.

Five of them were killed and more wounded; we suffered no casualties. The ambush position was right in the middle of Tourmakeady where the road bends sharply and a gateway enters a house. A flanking wall commands the house. We had a couple of fellows, good shots, placed there. They stopped it! There was a second lorry close behind. When it heard the shots it tried to stop, but it had already entered the ambush position. Some of them were hit too. One RIC man that was in it lost an arm and he died near here only very recently. Dismissing the local men we retired at once westward into the hills. It was not long until the chase was on. A few hours later, at about twelve o'clock, we were contacted by a party of British troops.

A running fight ensued. We withstood their attack with Lewis guns and rifle fire all day. There were two hundred and fifty or more of them, and of course they would have liked to out-flank and surround us. At one point I got hit. They were concentrating a terrible barrage on us just then my Adjutant, Michael O'Brien, crept over and tied me up, but I was still bleeding profusely. A party of them, led by a Lieut Ibberson, moved to outflank me. He was not in uniform his frock coat was off. He walked nonchalantly along, carrying a rifle, his bandolier across his white shirt. Suddenly taking aim he fired at O'Brien, who had just finished attending to me. He hit and fatally wounded O'Brien, who was in the act of picking up his rifle again, but at the same time, to my astonishment, I saw Ibberson collapse in shreds, his bandolier sliding off him, and his rifle falling to the ground as one of our lads got him. There was so much shooting and so much noise that I could not say where it came from, but it came from our side anyway, because there was a load of buckshot in it and it splattered all over Ibberson. He turned and ran; he could still run although his arms and body had pellets everywhere. When he turned up months afterwards in the court at Claremorris claiming damages, he still bore the scars.

Anyway, we held them off there for a day. It was a fine day in early summer, and unfortunately a long one. Crouched there in the fern, conserving our fire, we wondered if it would ever end. They pressed us very hard. A couple of us were wounded and one was killed. I had six bullet wounds, yet, strangely enough; I remained in full control of myself, and could stand up. As the hours crept by however, I became progressively weakened by the loss of blood and shock. I found I could scarcely raise myself to look around.

It was dark at last, and we had our first respite. Very lights shot into the air calling in the troops. We could hear the whistles too as they made their way back to the twenty-four lorries that brought them. What a relief it was. We had possession of the field. I was carried upon one fellow's back, my arms hanging down. The first house they came to I was brought in and laid down. I was comfortable there, but feeling very weak. Very early in the morning two Volunteers arrived.

Are you able to move, they asked? I had never taken spirits before, but that morning I was given a double egg flip mixed with whiskey and it did me a power of good. Leaning heavily upon both of them, I left the house and moved towards the end of the gable. Rounding it, there came a puff of wind, which flattened me. My legs buckled, I could travel no further. The British were everywhere, searching for stragglers such as myself. Still there was nothing for it but to return to the cottage.

At the time there was a doctor in Tourmakeady who had informed our lads that if ever he was needed he could be called upon. A message was conveyed to him by some youngster, and he came at once, but of course he could not bring anything with him. He rummaged around the house, picking up a few sceilphs of wood, and some bits of wool, and a clean flour bag. With these he improvised the necessary splints and bandages. I was inside that cordon from Tuesday until the Saturday night. They were unable to move me out of it; neither could they leave me in the house. I had to be moved away outside and left in the bracken. On the Tuesday, it was a Holy day, I remember, they were again carrying me early up the hill to place me in a hollow, and I could feel the trees and bushes striking the shawl they wrapped me in. At the same time an aeroplane came in low, so low it would deafen you, but it passed on. They left me in this hollow anyway, and retired down again. They had scarcely gone when it commenced to pour rain. In a short while I was soaked through. I don't know if you have ever lain soaked through, but if it is not too cold it can almost be a pleasurable experience. While I lay like that I could hear the soldiers about me, methodically criss-crossing their steps. I was as near as that, but they did not find me. At long last, in the evening the whistles were blown again, and I could hear the sound of the lorries starting up. They got me out on the Saturday night.

Appendix D – Telegram sent by Lt Ibberson on receipt of the call-out (*The Border Magazine*).

1. To O.C. Military Barracks, Castlebar.
    Hellfire Tourmakeady AAA Ballinrobe Srah Tourmakeady
    AAA Castlebar Killavally Bohaun Ravine Tourmakeady AAA.
    From: Military Ballinrobe.

2. To: O.C. RIC Barracks Westport
    Hellfire Tourmakeady AAA Ballinrobe Srah Tourmakeady.
    AAA Westport Winding Valley Tourmakeady AAA.
    From Military Ballinrobe.

Explanation of Telegrams:

1. Hellfire Tourmakeady – Ambush at Tourmakeady. Ballinrobe Srah
    Tourmakeady – the route by which the senders of the telegram,
    i.e. ourselves were to proceed to the scene of the ambush.
    Castlebar Killavally Bohaun Ravine Tourmakeady – the route
    by which recipients of the telegram should proceed to the scene
    of the ambush.

2. Similar to above.[158]

Appendix E – Notes by Major Ibberson MBE Sept 1956. (*The Border Magazine*).

This story, which might well have the alternative title "Muddling Through" (rather than 'The Tourmakeady Affair') was first written in May, 1921, that is as soon as my right hand came back to life. The manuscript has been in the bank with my will for a long time. It would still be there but for Mr Goulden. In May, 1921, 2nd Battalion, the Border Regiment was stationed in the West of Ireland and "C" Company occupied the military barracks at Ballinrobe. Royal Irish Constabulary were also stationed in the town.

I vaguely remember the son of one of the R.I.C. sergeants because he used to watch our football games and play "kick about" with the soldiers on the green beside the barracks. He was then thirteen years old. Later at Trinity College, Dublin, he was a "rugger man." Now he is a schoolmaster, historian and archaeologist. One evening in May, 1955, this gentleman, Mr J.R.W. Goulden rang me up from Dublin, and it is he who is really responsible for this article being written. I must add, however, that the editor also wishes it to be recorded in this journal.

Here I will mention that Thomas Maguire, "O.C., Mayo South, Irish Republican Army," also wrote a report of the Tourmakeady affair dated 4th June 1921, and dispatched it to "A.G., G.H.Q., I.R.A.," Dublin. This report was captured by troops of the Leicestershire Regiment when they held up and searched the Galway Mail train at Athlone. The engine driver had it, I was told. A copy of this report was given to me in hospital in Dublin. It amused us at the time. Like many reports by guerrillas it was a tangle of inaccuracies, vain imaginings, and extravagant claims. I kept this also in the bank with my will.

In the course of considerable correspondence with Mr Goulden, whose chief historical interest is to get at the truth, he sent me copies of three publications dealing with the Tourmakeady affair. All are based on Thomas Maguire's report. I was unaware of these publications. Also within recent months an account has been published in serial form in the *Sunday Press*, a Dublin Newspaper.

In one book, *The Red Path to Glory*, published by Kerryman Ltd., on page 221, Mr Edward Gallagher heads his article, 'Thirty I.R.A. Men Defied 600 British Troops at Tourmakeady,' and the Border Regiment is mentioned. In fact, only two officers and eight soldiers saw or even knew of the whereabouts of Thomas Maguire's I.R.A. column in the Partry Mountains above Tourmakeady much before nightfall on that day, 3rd May, 1921. In Maguire's original report the casualties inflicted on us soldiers vary between 40 (definite) and 55 (according to report). I was the only military casualty! Again, when I ran into the rebels at close quarters, thereby surprising them and to some extent myself, I happened to be alone. All their accounts give me eight soldiers. These, apparently, whilst I was shooting and being shot, 'fumbled with their rifles and subsequently fled'! They were also 'caught between the fire of my men and their own guns and six of them fell'. Perhaps best of all Maguire writes: 'The enemy never attempted until the next day to attend to their wounded or take their dead off the hills'.

Appendix F – Major Ibberson MBE. Letter to the *Sunday Press*, 18 December 1955.

The recent articles in your paper by Mr O'Malley on the Ambush at Tourmakeady on 3rd May, 1921, and the subsequent action in the Partry Hills calls for comment. The story is based on a report written by T. Maguire (O.C. Mayo South), dated 4th June, 1921. This report was captured by the British Military at Athlone. I have a copy. The report as applied to British troops, was a tangle of inaccuracies and vain imaginations which appear to increase with the telling.

One cannot blame those writers. They have to rely on hearsay, whereas I was present and also planned the action against Maguire's column. My account in detail has been submitted to the Bureau of Military History and the libraries of Trinity College and the Royal Irish Academy. The following salient facts should however be known:

1. A maximum of two officers and twenty soldiers ever got within two miles of Maguire's column in the Partry Hills.
2. The only casualty inflicted by Maguire's column that day were four R.I.C. killed and two wounded and myself wounded.
3. I was alone at the place where O'Brien died. There were no eight soldiers "fumbling with their rifles" and subsequently to flee.
4. The following weapons discarded by the column were I understand, collected near O'Brien's body the next day, 4th May, 8 rifles, 1 revolver, 20 shotguns.

Finally may I pay tribute to O'Brien? He came about 20 yards out of cover to bring back the wounded Maguire. He came out a second time to collect a weapon left at the spot where Maguire fell. Thirdly, he took a snap shot at me and did not raise his hands like many others when called upon to surrender.

Appendix G – Maguire's Fourth Report. Reply to Ibberson *Sunday Press*, 8 January 1956.

Mr. Ibberson endeavours to give the impression that he was present while the action in the hills lasted. He was not. He was not present at the ambush at Tourmakeady and knows nothing about it beyond what he has learned from hearsay. In the fight in the hills Ibberson became a casualty at a comparatively early stage and was out of the fight for the greater part of the day. He made his way down to the house of Patrick Lydon of Tour-na-bhFod. There his wounds were dressed by the occupants of the house and Mr Lydon later carted him to the British base on the main road.

This is the man who has the presumption to give an account of the day's happenings "in detail has been submitted to the bureau of Military History and the libraries of Trinity College and the Royal Irish Academy." Those bodies could have got his "account" word for word by reference to Dublin Castle's "Weekly Summary" of that period. What a valuable source of historical data!

Since he has added some fanciful matter regarding "the wounded Maguire" to his letter to The Sunday Press and has now for the first time produced his twenty soldiers and two officers. On the other hand the IRA report was written by the man who planned, organised and led the attack on the British forces both at the ambush and in the hills. He did not withdraw from the fight at any time. He maintained control of his unit, though wounded, until the firing of the last shot and was the last man to leave the field. His report to his Headquarters contained the main facts, merely of the day's work. In any account since given or recorded of the events of that day, nothing has been added or taken from that report by him. It will take more than Ibberson's statement of "vain imaginings" and "tangle of inaccuracies" to explain away the failure of a force of seasoned British troops numerically superior in the proportion of ten to one and incomparably superior in armament to annihilate or capture an IRA unit some of whom were armed only with shotguns.

"A maximum of two officers and twenty soldiers ever got within two miles of Maguire's column in the Partry hills" he says. There is evidence of the local people of Mount Partry and of those living along the roads travelled by the British on that day on their way to the scene of activities to prove him wrong. I counted twenty-four vehicles approaching along one road, and I did not get them all.

The parked vehicles standing fairly close together extended from Srah Post Office over a distance of three-quarters of a mile of road. Does Mr Ibberson expect us to believe that the British authorities sent the large concentration of men carried by these vehicles out for a ride? Or does he insinuate that the comrades-in-arms hung back in the face of the enemy and sent him forward alone to fight the Empire's battle?

Making due allowance for the reluctance of the British soldiers, as implied by him, to come to grips with the IRA, zealous officers could have got the troops over those two miles to the IRA position in a maximum time of about one hour. In fact they had almost a day in which to do it. Were they to travel at a fifth of the speed at which Ibberson and his party took their departure from that position they would have got there very much under the hour. The truth is that the troops were sent into action immediately they were got off the lorries. They had the IRA where they always wanted them–in the open. The opportunity was too good to be missed or wasted. There was no cover in the generally accepted meaning of the term, which the IRA could have availed themselves. There was no timber, no bush, no scrub, no hedges, ditch or wall, just the bleak open hillside. The day was dry and visibility perfect. The British did not even have the disadvantage of operating against a force of unknown strength.

In a running fight while they were being manoeuvred into the best defensive position, the Irish were fully exposed to view. Though under heavy rifle fire they suffered no casualties in that encounter. Having got into that position, the IRA were quickly making full use of the depression and irregularities in the ground which sloped gently away from a slight eminence on the left flank, occupied by the Column Commander, to the right flank occupied by Commandant O'Brien, South Mayo Brigade Adjutant. The unequal contest was soon in full progress. Rifle and shotgun on one side, rifle, Lewis machine-gun and unlimited ammunition on the other. The terrified horses, cattle and sheep and even the hares raced away from the maddening noise.

The English had the range to a nicety now, and poured in a deluge of lead in what we knew was intended to be a softening up process prior to an assault. In due course, having completed the softening-up to their satisfaction, Ibberson was ordered forward with his party. Expecting, presumably, as we were forced under the terrific barrage to keep down, to find very little life and no fight among the IRA, he stripped for action. Divesting himself of his cap, belt and coat and arming himself with a rifle and bandolier, he advanced under the protection of a heavy covering fire, dressed only in breeches and shirt, to our left flank. He states in his letter that he was alone. In so far as he was slightly in advance of his party, he was. When they came close enough to prevent the waste of any valuable ammunition on our part, as the day was still young, they were fired on and beaten off, Ibberson leaving his rifle and bandolier behind him. As I have already stated, he fled from the scene and had no further part in the fight. Unfortunately Comdt O'Brien went down in that affray. Ibberson has the effrontery now to pose as an admirer of Comdt O'Brien's courage on that occasion when, in actual fact, he fired at Comdt O'Brien when he was at a definite disadvantage.

A few day's later at Comdt O'Brien's funeral, the conduct of Ibberson's colleagues among the gentlemen of the British army was anything but creditable to that army. "May I pay tribute to O'Brien. He came out about twenty yards out of cover to bring back the wounded Maguire. He came out a second time to collect a weapon at the spot where Maguire fell. Thirdly he took a snap shot at me and did not raise his hands like many others when called upon to surrender," writes Mr Ibberson. Nothing so dramatic as the carrying back to cover of the wounded Maguire took place. There was no cover to which to be carried. Furthermore Maguire had not fallen. Even when hit a second time that day he did not fall. There was no collecting of a dropped weapon and to say that any man there put up his hands is absolutely untrue. Before the attempt to carry our position, I got hit.

Running the gauntlet of the enemy's terrific fire, Comdt O'Brien came the full length of our position to assist me. Crouching low to avoid the hail of bullets from a Lewis gun that ripped into the ground within a few feet of him and sent the heather and the turf flying in a shower over him, he worked hurriedly to staunch the flow of blood. He was kneeling at my side and behind me when Ibberson came on the scene and aimed at him. Comdt O'Brien's rifle had been laid on the ground, he snatched it up and aimed, but he was hit before he could fire.

Ibberson makes a statement, learned second-hand to the effect that rifles and shotguns were found by the British on the following day. I deny that. The statement is so silly as to be beneath notice. The IRA defended their positions against heavy odds from 2 o'clock in the afternoon until the darkness of night descended on the hills. The English had withdrawn under cover of darkness having failed to achieve their objective. Was it likely that the men who had inflicted a decisive defeat on their and their country's enemies and who had been left in possession of the field would discard their arms?

There are many memories of that days fighting carefully preserved in South Mayo. Not the least interesting of those are Ibberson's rifle and bandolier and a rifle through the butt of which a bullet was sent to its billet in a Britisher as he was in the act of firing. The IRA members who took part in the actions at Tourmakeady and

Carraig-an-Tom-Shailligh (scene of the fight in the hills) had been through a period of intensive training under the personal care of the man who would lead them in their encounters with the enemy. In addition to the usual training special practice was given in the use of cover and they had instilled into their minds the fact that, with the short range weapons and limited supply of ammunition available to them, all their fights would be at close quarters.

Consequently, when up against the real thing in the open, they were steady and resourceful. They also had impressed on them the fact that man for man they were superior to anything that England could put in the field against them. They proved that they were. Living and sleeping in the open since the previous February, the men were in the peak of physical condition, strong, lithe and tough. Their morale was exceptionally high. Without the aid of roadblocks, those boys could stop the speeding motor vehicles of the British armed forces and did so with complete success when the occasion demanded. Their display of grit, fighting spirit and chivalrous loyalty to their wounded leader on May 3, 1921, has few parallels even in that brave time.

Appendix H – Tourmakeady 3rd of May 1921

"We're off to Tourmakeady boys,"
Our leader then did say,
"For another blow to crush the foe
and clear them far away".

When we first skirted the Partry hills
'Twas early in the Spring
And round the mountain far and wide
We formed in a ring.

The English were determined
That O'Brien should never fight,
And every day throughout the year
They searched for him far and wide.

He first tested their mettle
At the battle of Port Royal,
When the South Mayo Flying Column
Fought to reverse the English smile.

"Hands up" cried Captain Emerson
But he proudly answered "No",
And he fell for Irish freedom
As he blazed the Saxon foe.

We lost one man, God rest his soul,
From earth he passed away;
He was a noble soldier
Of the famous IRA.

His name was Michael O'Brien
From the parish of the Neale.
The Lord have mercy on his soul
And grant old Ireland freedom.

We gained that day in victory,
And left them lying low
And we let them know we're the IRA
From the County of Mayo.

Appendix I – Cath Tuar Mhic Éadaigh.

Ar maidin Dé Máirt an chnoc Thuar na bhFód,
Chuala mé an bubhall seidte,
Bhí pudar's gran is pileir go leor,
A gcaitheadh ar dhroim na sleibhte.
Gan magadh na greann tháinig pian i mo cheann,
'S mo chuid fola ag dul thrí na chéile,
Cur shíleas ar ndó nach mbeadh aon nduine beo,
As seo go Tuar Mhic Éadaigh.

Tríd Dhoire Mhór tháinig go leor
D'arm Shéain Bhú gan fáilte,
Nár bhfearr dhóibh ag ól i Liverpool thall,
Na ar mhullach na sleibhte fagtha,
Dúirt oifigeach mór a bhí dilís don choróin
Nach bhfagfadh sé beo mac máthair
Ach chuaigh pillirí luaidh ina phutóga broghach,
'S ní fhéic fidhear é aris san áit seo.

Tháinig eagla ar mo chroi 's é á tíocht chun mo thí,
Ag iarraidh na dí 's é ag pleascadh,
Ach bhí sean canna stain amuigh ar an tsráid
'S thug mé deoch do as linn na ngeabha.
D'Agair sé arís go bhfaighinn rud eigin mín
Le cur ar a chroí is plastar
Ach fuair mé ceamhas den líon a raibh deilgne thríd,
'S nar dhoiligh dhó an óiche a sharú.

Ar dhroim Raith an Óir bhí an briseadh ba mhó,
Ag caitheamh ar lom an tséidte,
Ach ag tíocht an trathnóna bhí muidne ag ghnóthachan,
'S na saighduiri granna feachta.
Mas Sasannach é nó fear as South Wales,
B'fearr do nach bhfeicfeadh sé an áit seo,
Ní raibh aige le fáil ach pudar 's gran,
Nár chruaidh iad le dhu ina chaoille.

Ar an Leargan lom gan claí gan chaoilicí tom,
Sea chuala mé glaoch an "Sinn Féiner"
"Buailligí go cruaidh 's na failligí an uair
Beidh againne an lá ar aon chor."
Is gairid gur ghluais na Sasannaigh anuas,
Ag tiomáint go gear ar Éirinn,
'S ar LLoyd George a chur lad anall,
Ag cumhdach poilios da mb'féidir.

Saol fada le séan ag na buachaillí trean,
A rinne ár gcás a reiteach,
'S a dhibhir fir Sheáin as Éire go brach,
Ba surach e a ndí is a mbeasa.
Se an "Volunteer" a chruthaigh go fíor
'S a choinnigh a chuid fear le chéile,
Nár fhágaí sa tír aon bhearic poilios,
'S dheamhain cleite acu i dTuar Mhic Éadaigh.

Michael O hÉanachain (Curly), Gortbhun a' Chuillin,
Tuar Mhic Éadaigh

Appendix J – The Partry Mountains.

Along the Party Mountains we had a dreadful day
In wars we were surrounded all upon the 3rd of May
My mind it was completely gone, it seemed to me a dream
That bullets flew like hailstones at Bealamoondian stream.

Thully Ard and Karran are now on record
Our heroes won the battlefield, all praise to the Lord
They fought like loyal Irishmen along the mountainside,
May God protect them every day, and always be their guide.

The bullets they were whizzing round flying like the hail
I often heard success favours the sons of Granuale
They drove away the enemy in terror they did go
Which yields a lot of credit to the boys of South Mayo.

At the top of Garry Eamonn it would grieve your heart full sore
To see the soldiers raiding the side of Krodan More
But fortune proved unkind to them as one of them got a pill
A mighty bold Sinn Feiner was close behind the hill.

Upon the side of Laragon, the volunteers did say
Cheer up my gallant countrymen, it's now we have won the day
The soldiers we have conquered on the slopes of Rainanor
God is on the run with us and will for evermore.

It's now we join in praise to thank the Lord on high
That saved the proud Sinn Feiners when danger it was neigh
They proved themselves St. Patrick's sons no danger did they fear
Long live the Tourmakeady boys and the Irish Volunteers.

The volunteers were everywhere successful on that day
Excepting poor O'Brien who fell all in the fray
He died for dear old Ireland, the bravest of the brave
May the Lord have mercy on his soul he lies in his grave.

Michael Heneghan (1921)

Bibliography

Primary Sources

1. Manuscript Sources

Military Archives – Bureau of Military History 1947-1957

WS 872
File No. S. 2166
Witness: Thomas Ketterick, Howth County Dublin
ID QM West Mayo Brigade, ASU West Mayo Brigade
Subject: National and military activities West Mayo, 1915-1921

WS 927
File No. S. 2236
Witness: Sean Gibbons, Dollymount, Dublin
ID Adjutant West Mayo Brigade 1921
Subject: National and military activities in West Mayo 1912-1921

WS 1735
File No. S. 3042
Witness: P.J. (Paddy) Kelly, Westport

ID OC Louisburgh Battalion
Subject: Louisburgh Company
  Louisburgh Battalion IRA 1917-Truce

WS 1668
File No. S. 2928
Witness: Thomas Hevey, Ballina, County Mayo
ID Brigade Adjutant, West Mayo Brigade
Subject: West Mayo Brigade IRA 1919-1921

WS 896
File No. S. 2195
Witness: Edward Moane, Oldtown, Dublin
ID Member of IRB Westport 1911-. Adjutant Westport Battalion,
IRA, Vice Commandant West Mayo Brigade IRA
Subject: National and Military activities, West Mayo 1919-1921

WS 1340
File No. S. 2669
Witness: Mr J.R.W. Goulden, Glasnevin, Dublin
ID Son of Sgt Goulden RIC who was stationed at Tourmakeady,
County Mayo in 1921
Subject: Tourmakeady ambush, County Mayo, 3rd May 1921, and
events immediately preceding it.

WS 1307.
File No. S. 2655
Witness: Major Geoffrey Ibberson MBE, Winterbourne Earls,
Salisbury, England
ID Lieutenant, The Border Regiment, 1921

Subject: The Tourmakeady ambush, County Mayo, 3rd May, 1921

University College Dublin – Ernie O'Malley Papers.
National Library Ireland – *Sunday Press.*
Mayo, County Library, Castlebar - British in Ireland Police
    Reports.
Imperial War Museum, London –Lieutenant General SirHugh
    Jeudwine Papers.
Border & King's own Royal Border Regiment Museum, Carlisle
    - 2 Battalion Digest of Service.
The Border Magazine.

2. Printed Sources

Newspapers
The Times
The Irish Times
Irish Independent
The Mayo News
The Western People
The Connacht Tribune
Saoirse

Contemporary Periodicals
The London Gazette
An tÓglach

3. Interviews

Peter McGoldrick (5 March, 2007).
Joan Ó'hEánacháin (10 July, 2007).
Tomás Ó'hEánacháin (10 July, 2007).
Tomás Ó'Toole (17 July, 2007).

4. Secondary Sources

Abbot, R., *Police Casualties in Ireland* (Mercier Press: Cork, 2000).
Augusteijn, J., *From Public Defiance to Guerrilla Warfare* (Irish Academic Press: Dublin, 2006).
Crozier, F. P., *Ireland For Ever* (Cedric Chivers Ltd: Bath, 1971).
Crozier, F. P., *The Men I Killed* (Athol Books Ltd: Belfast, 2002).
Duff, D.V., *Sword for Hire* (Butler and Tanner Ltd: London, 1934).
Gallagher, E., *The Red Path of Glory.* (Kerryman Ltd: Tralee, 1955).
Hart, P., *British Intelligence in Ireland 1920-1921* (Cork University Press: Cork, 2002).
Hopkinson, M., *The Irish War of Independence* (Gill & Macmillan Ltd: Dublin, 2002).
Kee, R., *Ourselves Alone* (Quartet Books: London, 1976).
Macardle, D., *The Irish Republic* (Irish Press Ltd: Dublin, 1951).
Mansergh M., *The Legacy of History* (Mercier Press: Cork, 2003).
McCann, J., *War by the Irish* (The Kerryman: Tralee, 1946).
Moran, G., *The Mayo Evictions* (FNT, : Westport, 1986).
Murphy, B., *The Origin & Organisation of British Propaganda in Ireland 1920* (Aubane Historical Society and Spinwatch: Millstreet, 2006).
O' Brádaigh, R., *Dílseacht* (Irish Freedom Press: Dublin, 1997).

O' Farrell, P., *Who's Who in the Irish War of Independence 1916-1923* (The Lilliput Press: Dublin, 1997).

Ó hÓgáin, S., 'The Tourmakeady Ambush May 1921 – Part 1' *Cathair na Mart* No 22 (Westport, 2002)

Ó hÓgáin, S., 'The Tourmakeady Ambush May 1921' – Part 2. *Cathair na Mart* No 23 (Westport, 2003).

O'Malley, E., *Memories of a Mayoman.* (FNT: Westport, 1981).

O'Malley, E., *Raids and Rallies.* (Anvil Books Ltd: Dublin, 1982).

'Cathair na Mart', *Cathair na Mart* No 26(Westport, 2006).

Endnotes

1. Hart, P., *British Intelligence in Ireland 1920-1921* (Cork University Press: Cork, 2002)p.77.

2. *A Report on the Intelligence Branch of the Chief of Police, Dublin Castle from May 1920 to July 1921.* PRO, WO/35/214.

3. Hopkinson, M., *The Irish War of Independence* (Gill & Macmillan Ltd: Dublin, 2002) p.128.

4. *Ibid.*

5. Kee, R., *Ourselves Alone* (Quartet Books: London, 1976). p.128.

6. Augusteijn, J., *From Public Defiance to Guerrilla Warfare* (Irish Academic Press: Dublin, 2006) p. 203.

7. *Digest of Service.* 1921-21. 2 Border Regiment. Regimental Museum Carlisle UK.

8. Mansergh M., *The Legacy of History* (Mercier Press: Cork, 2003)p.306.

9. O' Brádaigh, R., *Dílseacht* (Irish Freedom Press: Dublin, 1997).p.9.

10. Ó'hÓgáin, S., 'The Tourmakeady Ambush, May 1921' *Cathair na Mart 2002.*

11. Colleran, J., *Waterfall* (Tourmakeady Parish 1992) pp.7-11.

12. O'Malley, E., *Memories of a Mayoman* (FNT: Westport, 1981).

13. O'Malley, E., *Raids and Rallies* (Anvil Books Ltd: Dublin, 1982).

14. Goulden, J.W.R., *Statement* 1956. BMH, WS No. 1340. p.6.

15. *Cathair na Mart*, 21. 'Discovered document'. Source unknown. p.158.

16. Moran, G., *The Mayo Evictions* (Nonsuch Publishing,: Dublin 2007). p.24.

17. *The Mayo News*, 24 June 1905.

18. Goulden, *Statement,* p.6.

19 PRO. RIC Files. CO / 940 / 149-150.

20. Abbot, R., *Police Casualties in Ireland* (Mercier Press: Cork, 2000)p.89.

21. Goulden, *Statement*, p.6.

22. *Ibid.*

23. *Digest of Service.* 1920-21. The Border Regiment.

24. *Ibid.*

25. Mac Eoin, U., *Survivors,* (Argenta Publications: Dublin, 1980) pp. 383-4.

26. *Ibid.*

27. Ó hÓgáin, S., 'The Tourmakeady Ambush'. C na M, No 22, 2002. Part 1, p. 50.

28. Maguire, T., 'The Battle of Tourmakeady' *An tÓglach*, GHQ IRA 19 Aug 1921. pp. 2-3.

29. Goulden, p.8.

30. O'Malley, *Raids and Rallies*, p.118.

31. Maguire.

32. Mac Eoin, pp. 283-4.

33. Ó hÓgáin, 'Tourmakeady Ambush', Part 1, p.50.

34. Ó hÓgáin is drawing on a talk in 1966 given by Pat Kennedy, a veteran of the ambush.

35. O'Malley, *Raids and Rallies*, p.119.
36. Ó hÓgáin, 'Tourmakeady Ambush', Part 1, p.50.
37. Mac Eoin, p.284.
38. *Ibid.*
39. Ó hÓgáin, 'Tourmakeady Ambush', Part 1, p. 50.
40. Goulden, p.8.
41. O'Malley, *Raids and Rallies*, p.133.
42. Goulden, p.9.
43. Mac Eoin, p.285.
44. O'Malley, *Raids and Rallies*, p.120.
45. Ó hÓgáin, 'Tourmakeady Ambush', Part 1, pp.56-57.
46. *Ibid.*
47. Joan Ó'hEánacháin (10 July 2007).
48. O'Malley, *Raids and Rallies*, p.120.
49. Ó'hÓgáin, 'The Tourmakeady Ambush' Part 1, p.54.
50. Maguire.
51. O'Malley E., Papers, IE UCDA P17. p.151.
52. Mac Eoin, p. 287.
53. Maguire.
54. *Ibid.*
55. O'Malley, *Raids and Rallies*, p.121.
56. Macardle, D., *The Irish Republic* (Irish Press Ltd: Dublin, 1951) p.440.
57. Maguire.
58. O'Malley, *Raids and Rallies*, p.122.
59. Macardle, *The Irish Republic*, p.440.
60. Ó'hÓgáin, 'The Tourmakeady Ambush', Part 1, p.55.
61. Mac Eoin, p.285.
62. O'Malley, *Raids and Rallies*, p.122.
63. O'Malley, *Raids and Rallies*. p.123.

64. Macardle, p.441.

65. O'Malley, *Raids and Rallies*, p.123.

66. Macardle, p.441.

68. *Ibid.*

69. *Ibid.*

70. O'Malley, *Memories of a Mayoman,* p.49.

71. Maguire.

72. *Ibid.*

73. Mac Eoin, p.286.

74. Macardle, p.441.

75. Maguire.

76. O'Malley, *Raids and Rallies,* p.127.

77. *Ibid*, p.129.

78. Mac Eoin, p.286.

79. At this stage of the War of Independence aircraft were being used for reconnaissance. However, Galway Brigade requested that co-operating aircraft carry bombs and machine guns. This request was denied by GHQ but permission was later granted towards the end of May 1921. Jeudwine. *History of 5 Div in Ireland Nov 1919-Mar 1922.* p.104.

81. Ó hÓgáin, 'The Tourmakeady Ambush' Part 1, p.57.

82. O'Malley, *Memories of a Mayoman,* (FNT: Westport, 1981), p.50.

83. O'Malley, *Raids and Rallies,* p.131.

84. O'Malley, *Raids and Rallies,* p.128.

85. Moane, E., *Statement,* 1953 BMH, WS No. 896. p.18.

86. Ketterick, T., *Statement,* 1953. BMH, WS No. 872. pp. 28-29.

87. Hevey, T., *Statement,* 1957. BMH, WS No. 1668. p.139.

88. Maguire.

90. Ó hÓgáin, 'The Tourmakeady Ambush', Part 2, p.50.

91. Macardle, p.441.

92. O'Malley, *Memories of a Mayoman,* p.48-49

93. Mac Eoin, p.286.

94. Maguire, 'The Battle of Tourmakeady'.

95. Macardle, p. 441.

96. O'Malley, *Memories of a Mayoman,* p.39.

97. *Sunday Press,* 3 Jan 1956, p.2.

98. *Ibid.*

99. *Saoirse,* Aug 1993, pp.7-9.

100. *Ibid.*

101. *Ibid.*

102. Ibberson. *The Border Magazine* September 1956. The King's Own Royal Border Regiment Museum. Carlisle.

103. John McCann. *War by the Irish,* (Tralee: Kerryman. 1956), pp. 194-195 and Edward Gallagher, *The Red Path to Glory* (Tralee: Kerryman) p.213.

104. *Sunday Press* (20/11/1955, 27/11/1955, 4/12/1955).

105. Lt Gen Sir Hugh Jeudwine Papers. *13869/G History of 5 Division in Ireland Nov-Mar 1922* and *Record of Rebellion in Ireland and the part played by the Army in dealing with it. Volume 1 Operations* Imperial War Museum, London.

106. Goulden, p.10.

107. *Ibid*, p.11.

108. *Ibid.*

109. Jeudwine, *History of 5 Division in Ireland, March 1919 - November 1922.* p.91.

110. Ibberson, *Statement*, p.2.

111. Ibberson, *The Border Magazine*, p.33.

112. Ibberson, *Statement*, p.8.

113. Ibberson, *The Border Magazine*, p.32.

114. Ibberson, *Statement,* p.8.
115. Ibberson, *Statement,* p.10.
116. Ibberson, *The Border Magazine,* p.33.
117. *Ibid.*
118. *Ibid.*
119. *Ibid.*
120. *Ibid.*
121. *Ibid.*
123. *The Border Magazine.*
124. *Ibid.*
125. *Ibid.*
126. Goulden, *Statement,* p.13.
127. *The Irish Times*, 7 May 1921.
128. *Ibid.*
129. *Irish Independent,* 6 May 1921.
130. *Irish Independent,* 6 May 1921.
131. *The Western People,* 7 May 1921.
132. *Ibid.*
133. *The Times,* 6 May 1921.
134. *The Connacht Tribune,* 9 May 1921.
135. *Ibid,* 14 May 1921.
136. *The Mayo News,* 28 May 1921.
137. Jeudwine, 13869/G, History of the 5th Division in Ireland Nov '19 to Mar '22. Personal papers. Imperial War Museum. London.
138. *The Western People,* 5 Nov 1921.
139. *The Western People,* 5 Nov 1921.
140. *The Western People,* 5 Nov 1921.
141. *The Times,* 6 Feb 1929.
142. *Ibid,* 13 Dec 1933.

143. *The Times*, 27 April 1933.

144. *Ibid*, 13 April 1927.

145. *Ibid*, 25 Feb 1931.

146. *Ibid*, 8 May 1949.

147. Peter McGoldrick, 5 March 2007.

148. *The London Gazette*, 28 Sept 1921.

149. Lt Gen Sir Hugh Jeudwine, GOC 5 Division. Private Papers, *Record of Rebellion in Ireland. Volume 1 Operations.* p.61.

150. *Ibid*.

151. Peter McGoldrick, 5 March 2007.

152. Lt Gen Sir Hugh Jeudwine, GOC 5 Division. Private Papers, *Record of Rebellion in Ireland. Volume 1 Operations,* Appendix 2, p.61.

153. Mac Eoin.

154. Ibberson, *Statement*.

155. Duff, *Sword for Hire* (Butler & Tanner: London, 1934) p.82.

156. *Ibid*, p.77.

157. *Ibid*, p.78.

158. Ibberson, *Statement*, pp.3-4.

Index